In the Struggle:
Memoirs from Grodno and the Forests

PREVIOUSLY PUBLISHED IN THIS SERIES BY YAD VASHEM:

Enzo Tayar, *Days of Rain*

Alan Elsner, *Guarded by Angels: How My Father and Uncle Survived Hitler and Cheated Stalin*

Isabelle Choko, Frances Irwin, Lotti Kahana-Aufleger, Margit Raab Kalina, Jane Lipski, *Stolen Youth: Five Women's Survival in the Holocaust*

Hadassah Rosensaft, *Yesterday, My Story*

Gabriel Mermall, Norbert J. Yasharoff, *By the Grace of Strangers: Two Boys' Rescue During the Holocaust*

E.H. (Dan) Kampelmacher, *Fighting for Survival*

Hersch Altman, *On the Fields of Loneliness*

Flora M. Singer, *Flora, I was but a Child*

Israel Cymlich, Oskar Strawczynski, *Escaping Hell in Treblinka*

Moty Stromer, *Memoirs of an Unfortunate Person: the Diary of Moty Stromer*

Menachem Katz, *Path of Hope*

PUBLISHED BY THE UNITED STATES HOLOCAUST MEMORIAL MUSEUM:

Adam Boren, *Journey Through the Inferno*

Margaret Bergmann Lambert, *By Leaps and Bounds*

Joseph E. Tenenbaum, *Legacy and Redemption: A Life Renewed*

In the Struggle:
Memoirs from Grodno and the Forests

LEIB REIZER

YAD VASHEM AND
THE HOLOCAUST SURVIVORS' MEMOIRS PROJECT
New York • Jerusalem

Copyright © 2009 by Leib Reizer.

All rights reserved, including the right to reproduce this book or portions thereof in any form.

This book is published by Yad Vashem, the Holocaust Martyrs' and Heroes' Remembrance Authority, c/o American Society for Yad Vashem, 500 Fifth Avenue, 42nd floor, New York, New York 10110-4299, and P.O.B. 3477, Jerusalem 91034, Israel

www.yadvashem.org

and

The Holocaust Survivors' Memoirs Project
in association with the World Federation of Bergen-Belsen Associations, Inc.

The Holocaust Survivors' Memoirs Project, an initiative of Nobel Peace Prize laureate Elie Wiesel, was launched through a generous grant from Random House, Inc., New York, New York.

Cover photos and all other photographs courtesy of Leib Reizer.

Library of Congress Cataloging-in-Publication Data

Reizer, Leib, 1910-1986
In the struggle : memoirs from Grodno and the forests / by Leib Reizer.
p. cm.
  ISBN 0-9814686-2-4 (978-0-9814686-2-4 : alk. paper)
  1. Reizer, Leib, 1910-1986 2. Jews--Belarus--Hrodna--Biography. 3. Holocaust, Jewish (1939-1945)--Belarus--Hrodna--Personal narratives. 4. Hrodna (Belarus)--Biography. I. Title.
 DS135.B383R457 2009
 940.53'18092--dc22
 [B]
 2009019692

Typesetting: Judith Sternberg
Produced by Offset Nathan Shlomo Press

Printed in Jerusalem, Israel.

Series Editor

David Silberklang

Managing Editor

Daniella Zaidman-Mauer

Project Coordinator

Gloria Golan

Editorial Board

Menachem Z. Rosensaft, Chairman

Yehuda Bauer	Dan Michman
Melvin Jules Bukiet	David M. Posner
Sam E. Bloch	Romana Strochlitz Primus
Nathan Cohen	Thane Rosenbaum
Eva Fogelman	Jean Bloch Rosensaft
Alfred Gottschalk	Robert Rozett
Israel Gutman	Avner Shalev
Bella Gutterman	Elan Steinberg
Hagit Lavsky	

TABLE OF CONTENTS

FOREWORD
by Sir Martin Gilbert 11

CHAPTER 1
The Beginning 15

CHAPTER 2
They Are Retreating 17

CHAPTER 3
On the Road to Minsk 29

CHAPTER 4
Russian Soldiers 55

CHAPTER 5
The Minsk Ghetto 65

CHAPTER 6
Finding a Way Back to Grodno 79

CHAPTER 7
Shtetlach on the Way 85

CHAPTER 8
Jewish Life under the Nazis in Grodno 101

CHAPTER 9
News and Rumors 105

CHAPTER 10
Moving into the Ghetto 111

CHAPTER 11
Jewish Youth in the Ghetto 117

CHAPTER 12
Aktionen in the Ghetto 121

CHAPTER 13
Hiding in the Ghetto 131

CHAPTER 14
Mourning the Dead 137

CHAPTER 15
New Year's Eve 1943 143

CHAPTER 16
Fleeing 153

CHAPTER 17
Conclusion of the Scroll of Nacza 163

CHAPTER 18
Life in the Forest 165

CHAPTER 19
Freedom 175

AFTERWORD
by Betty (Reizer) Broit 179

PHOTOS 185

Translated from the Yiddish by Dr. Haike Beruriah Wiegand
Historical Consultant: Sharon Kangisser-Cohen
Language Editor: Jeannette Friedman

DEDICATION

These memoirs are a gift to my dear wife Frumke, who saved our 5-year-old daughter, Bashele, from the Grodno Ghetto on February 7, 1943. I am writing these words with honor and respect for my wife. To save our lives, we walked hundreds of kilometers together, through forests and mud, during those unfortunate days and nights. May God grant that our grandchildren never know such terrible times and that they will watch over the Jewish land of Israel as if it is as precious to them as their own eyes.

Leib Reizer, January 1985
Ra'anana

FOREWORD

By Sir Martin Gilbert

Each Holocaust memoir is unique, as is the story of every individual survivor. The variety of experiences, the places and the people encountered on the way, survival itself, each adds to our still growing knowledge of that terrible time. Leib Reizer completed this memoir in 1948. It is dedicated to his wife Frumke, with whom he shared so much, and whose own story is an integral part of this book.

No one can read this memoir without tears and anger: tears at the suffering and torments inflicted on the Jews, and anger at the perpetrators and bystanders who had no human decency.

Leib Reizer was born in 1910, in the then Tsarist Russian town of Grodno. A carpenter, he was for six years, until the outbreak of World War II in 1939, the chairman of the Professional Association of Carpentry Workers in the city. Life was settled and calm. Polish antisemitism was vexatious but tolerable. Grodno was a city with strong Jewish and Zionist life. Four hundred years before the start of World War II a Jewish couple there are recorded as being about to leave for Jerusalem. Even then, the Jewish community was two hundred years old.

On the eve of war there were 21,159 Jews in Grodno, almost half the total population. Under Soviet rule between 1939 and 1941, the Jews of the city organized a clandestine route out of the country to Palestine. Leib Reizer was recruited into a Soviet work brigade, to build a shoe factory. Then, in June 1941, with the German invasion of the Soviet Union, the horrors of war came to Grodno. Leib Reizer begins his memoir with this dramatic event: as German warplanes bombed the city with savage intensity, bringing death and destruction, and the Jews sought safety by hiding in cellars, or fleeing eastward. The description of those first terrible hours is graphically told, a graphic scenario of chaos, fear, desperation and dwindling hope.

The great strength of this memoir is Leib Reizer's ability to give the reader a sense of the turmoil and tragedy of those times. The emotions shine through, raw and gripping in their intensity. Leaving his wife and tiny daughter in Grodno, he fled eastward — a journey recounted with vivid intensity, including a terrifying description of the bombing of the town of Lida, and heartrending encounters with other Jews on the run. Eventually he reached Minsk. In the ghetto there he had to wear a yellow star: his description of his feelings in doing so — like a criminal — are poignant.

After three months in the Minsk ghetto, Leib Reizer made his way back to Grodno, another journey that he describes with strong emotion and graphic images, including a harrowing description of wartime Vilna. In Grodno he rejoined his wife and daughter. For a year and a half they lived in the Grodno ghetto. This memoir contains an exceptionally powerful account of the conditions in the ghetto, including the rampages of "gangs of Polish hooligans," the Gestapo raids, and the steady march of death. He was also a witness to the savage destruction by the Germans of their Soviet prisoners of war.

When the deportations from Grodno — the first of them to Auschwitz - began in November 1942, Leib Reizer and his family went into hiding in a cellar. His description of the many narrow escapes from discovery makes the blood chill. In mid-January 1943, 10,000 Jews were rounded up and deported to Treblinka. Many were shot dead in the streets during the round up.

Leib Reizer, his wife and daughter, emerging from their hiding place, returned to the much-depleted ghetto. Here Jewish life was on the cusp of death: "The Angel of Death enjoyed himself in the ghetto," Leib Reizer writes, "and everyone felt his eerie breath." He was fortunate to be taken to work in the German military hospital. His description of the maimed and wounded German soldiers is another harrowing moment.

Back in the ghetto, and another hiding place, and another German round-up. Another 10,000 Jews were deported. Then came the opportunity to escape from the ghetto and join a Jewish partisan group in the forests. It was February 7, 1943. Leib Reizer took his wife and daughter out with them to the forests, with twenty-six other Grodno Jews. For the next year-and-a-half, they hid in the forests, wandered, foraged for food, and managed to survive, despite repeated German searches and local informers always ready to betray their hiding places. Leib Reizer's description of life in the forests is compelling in its poignant detail.

On July 9, 1944, Soviet soldiers reached the forest hideout: "The redeemers had arrived." Leib Reizer returned with his wife and daughter to Grodno, a shattered city, its Jewish life destroyed. When the war finally ended in May 1945, they made their way westward to the American Zone of Germany and a Displaced Persons camp. As these camps were slowly emptied, they went as far from Europe as they could — to New Zealand.

Everyone should read this remarkable memoir. It is harrowing, emotional and revealing and — as a story of Jewish survival — inspiring.

Martin Gilbert
London
December 14, 2008

CHAPTER 1

The Beginning

An earthquake with strong sounds of thunder woke me. The little wooden house at the edge of the town — where I lived with my family — was shaking and trembling like a house of cards. The day had hardly broken and infernal flashes of exploding aerial bombs constantly hit the ground, rising like pillars of dust, powerful as volcanoes. With their bright flashing fire they blinked and cut through the early morning gloom.

Frightened and upset, I stood at the window with my wife, gazing in astonishment into the distance, over the fields and gardens that lay beneath our window. I could not imagine how the great miracle of nature could still manifest itself — that the sky was such a pure blue, and that the red rays of the rising sun so magnificently adorned the sky just as they did every other day.

Where could such a storm with such thunderbolts come from so suddenly?

The fierce clamoring and howling came from the engines of scores of airplanes and revealed the mystery. They came like packs of wolves. This was not a natural catastrophe but a much worse calamity, and while we quickly understood what that meant, we looked at each other in fright and did not have the courage to utter the word 'war'. We instinctively feared it so much, yet to our greatest surprise, it suddenly and unexpectedly broke out between the night of June 21 and the morning of June 22, 1941.

Half-naked, I ran outside. The cool, early morning air wiped the last traces of sleep away from my face. My body trembled convulsively out of fear and astonishment. Our neighbors were standing in the courtyard, also half-naked, craning their necks toward the sky. In fear, they looked at the planes that hovered low in the sky, just above their heads, like a mob of sparrow hawks.

Those enraged birds of prey, with crosses on their wings, sowed death and destruction in the streets and alleys of the town. Undisturbed, they were free to have their fun in the sky. They performed various acrobatic tricks. They rose up high, extremely high in the sky, and then suddenly dropped down while discharging tiny little dots from their bellies with a melancholy whistling sound. The dots fell and became bigger and bigger, moving in a slanted line, one after the other, above our heads.

They fell in another street and lifted century-old walls up into the air together with people who did not manage to escape in time. Then they threw them back onto the ground, burying all those beneath the rubble who had looked for hiding-places in the cellars, and those, who in their mad confusion, ran to wherever their eyes led them. In running away they had all found death.

Every now and then, new waves of airplanes arrived and unloaded their deathly cargoes like a cruel wrath upon the old houses; upon old people and innocent inhabitants of the town. It was as if the pilots had made a terrible vow not to leave a stone standing, to finish off the town and all its inhabitants, like in Sodom.

People ran from the houses and hiding-places like flocks of frightened birds, from wherever a bomb had fallen, to look for a safer place. Beneath their feet, bricks were scattered; sheets of tin roofing had been ripped from houses; glass was shattered. Telegraph poles were overturned in a tangle of wires, and amidst all of this, in great panic, people were dragging the dead and wounded, leaving zigzagging trails of blood behind them. They filled the dusty, smoky air with their sorrowful screaming and groaning. It did not enter into anyone's head to ask about or even look at the victims — we were worried for our own lives.

That lovely June morning the Angel of Death spread wide his black wings above the beautiful, majestic town of Grodno on the banks of the Nieman River, and everything that was alive sensed his cold and eerie breath. The sun rose higher in the clear blue sky and like a powerful projector, lit up the gruesome panorama. On all sides, the town was burning.

CHAPTER 2

They Are Retreating

When it became a little quieter and the sky stopped pouring fire, armored cars — some empty, others full of military personnel from the border zone — started to move eastward through the burning streets. One phrase was heard from the armored cars: "Our troops are retreating!"

It thrust a knife into our hearts. What would become of us? Our mothers, our fathers, our wives and children? Where should we run? Were we really abandoned and forsaken, left at the mercy of Hitler's bandits, who would arrive at any moment? We had quite a realistic idea what the wild barbarians were doing to the Jews from the press and the refugees' stories we'd been hearing for years.

As swiftly as arrows, the armored cars moved through the town. Here and there they stopped. There were the terrified, pale faces of soldiers, some reserved and silent. Others let drop a few words of bitter resentment, "In the middle of the night the scoundrels attack, without any warning, laying everyone low. For the time being we have to retreat, but no matter, we will return."

These last words hit us like hammer blows to the head: "We must retreat."

And what should we do if and when they came back? Would they still find us?

Half-empty armored cars were instantly filled with Jews who wanted to save themselves before the pestilence arrived. People were clinging with all their might to the high sides of the cars, as if they were drowning. Red Army soldiers grabbed those who had just crept out of their hiding-places by their hands, their shoulders, and helped them into the vehicles. The passengers were empty-handed.

No one asked for permission and no one complained to the soldiers. The soldiers themselves understood quite well that the Jews had to run first, and that it was their human duty to help them. None of those on the run asked where the armored cars were going. It made no difference. What mattered was getting away as quickly as possible from the pestilence-to-come. And whatever was to come, one would deal with it later.

But where does one run and who could run? After all, the tens of thousands of Jews in town were not able to get into those few vehicles. And what did one do with the little babies and children, with the old fathers and mothers, with the women? What would become of them? It was as if one was bound by chains and rooted to the spot.

Others said, "So what? Whatever will happen to everyone, will happen to us."

"But people," I asked, "Have you lost your minds? Don't you sense the smell of death? Haven't you seen how within just a few hours these bandits have brought utter devastation to the town and to its defenseless inhabitants?"

"What does your resigned 'So what?' mean?"

"If you have arms and legs, then run! And if you don't want to run, pick up the rifles and automatic weapons lying around in the streets, the ones the soldiers threw away in their panic. Lie in wait with your wives and children — in the streets, courtyards and hiding-places — and start a terrible war with the enemy, who will be arriving soon. Fight tooth and nail, a war to the death, because it is all the same! If you stay here and don't flee, you will have to die — one day sooner or later."

People have eyes and do not hear; they have minds and do not understand. For a while, the storm calmed down and people's animal instincts took over. People, afraid of hunger, looted shops and bakeries. They grabbed and dragged everything they could lay their hands on to their broken houses — a garment, a shoe, a bottle of liquor, cigarettes, tobacco.

Caught up in the mass hysteria, I grabbed two loaves of bread from a bakery that had been broken into. For a while I ran around with them in my hands and then I threw them away. Some one running by picked them up, looked at me, grumbled and disappeared into the chaos.

Something kept gnawing at me, I could not keep my thoughts together, and I had lost my common sense, just like those who were breaking into the shops and dragging things home. I decided to go home, but for quite a long time I was lost in the familiar streets until I realized that I was not on the right road. Finally, I found my way.

I acted very strangely and wild that day. That afternoon squadrons of planes returned and wreaked more destruction and death upon the parts of the town that were not yet completely wiped out. The bombs plowed up the streets and houses. Why did they pick on us? What did they still want from us? Our soldiers were no longer anywhere to be seen. What did they want from innocent, unarmed townspeople?

People went back into hiding in the cellars and holes.

And I — may I be forgiven for this — put up a hammock between the two apple trees in our courtyard, stretched out, looked wild-eyed into the sky, and counted the planes.

A bomb dropped in another courtyard and carried away a black sheet of tin roofing that landed near me. That shook me out of my reverie and I realized it was not the best time to be lying in a hammock and counting planes, since a stray bomb could come my way and upset my arithmetic. I ran quickly, like someone hunted, down into the cellar — and while running, was almost killed on the steps. Soon another bomb struck, alarmingly close to our hiding-place, and it seemed we might be buried alive.

The cellar was in the middle of the courtyard, a few meters underground, built of bricks, with a brick ceiling. It had once been used for storing apples over the winters and now it was a bomb shelter for 30 people. It was dark and damp and the air stank. Slow dripping could be heard coming from the ceiling and the brick walls were covered with wet slime. It was truly a mass grave. I had no desire to stay in the cellar — my natural impulse was to head for the light and warmth outside.

People in the cellar hardly spoke — only briefly among themselves. Even the children felt the seriousness of the situation and were not playful, but sat in the corners with the composure of well-balanced adults, worried, with their heads bent. From time to time a question was heard. "What will become of us? Probably 'they' will arrive soon."

When they heard that, people instinctively trembled, understanding who that was, those "they" that "will arrive soon." That meant, "What shall I do?"

I thought, should I run away, while there is still time and it is not yet too late? Or should I remain here with everybody else and miss the boat? The question tormented me, gnawing at me, and I could not find a logical answer. If I did run away, what would become of my wife and my dear 5-year-old daughter, Bashele?

My eyes slowly got used to the darkness. In the gloom I saw the silhouettes of faces and the outlines of bodies. My wife had her head down, and was crying, sobbing and choking on her tears, and my little daughter, a model of endurance, sat quietly in my wife's arms, holding her little head tucked into her chest. She did not even ask for food. I looked at them from my corner, my heart frozen. My thoughts tortured me terribly and I could not find a solution.

I was balancing weights like a shopkeeper — weighing my thoughts and plans. If I run away with my family, how far could we run with a child in our arms in such a hailstorm of fire? If I abandoned my most beloved and dearest in that place, would I ever be able to forgive myself?

No, never! I would have them on my conscience my whole life long and would never be able to erase the mark of Cain, not even if I washed a thousand times.

If I ran from my dear wife and child like a coward, trembling and wishing only to save my own skin, that would be a betrayal, for I promised to love them. What kind of a man would I be if in a time of danger I abandoned them at the edge of the abyss?

The feelings in my heart were strange and unhappy from the ideas that tormented my conscience, and I could not find a clear way out. From time to time, I furtively glanced at them, and then lowered my eyes to the ground. My heart was breaking, and in my mind, the six years of our happy and peaceful life together flashed past as on a reel of film. Two contradictory viewpoints sneaked into my head, fighting each other ferociously.

On the one hand was the moral code, including my love and attachment to my wife and child, and on the other, the strict iron law of the animal struggle for survival.

The second idea slowly but surely gained the upper hand. There was no point in me sitting there. I needed to run, as long as it was not too late, and whatever was to come after that, one could deal with it later. For the time being — at least — I needed to leave town.

It became a bit quieter. I crept out of the cellar. The brightness of the day pierced my eyes like a knife. The western sun cast its streams of light into my face and the warm air outside revived my frozen limbs. A friend of mine ran toward me, then dragged me along by the sleeve: "Come! Let's run! As long as it's not too late. Every minute is precious!"

In despair I screamed into the cellar, calling out my wife's name. She came out, looking pale, tear-stained, leading our child by the hand. She walked towards me with measured steps, looked straight into my face, as if she had understood my devilish plan. Her eyes were frightened and tear-swollen, as if they were imploring me: "Come, let us die together…"

Our conversation was short. I was the first to start: "I have to run away," I said it sharply and ruthlessly. She looked at me with her tear-swollen, imploring eyes. "No, don't run away! Let's stay together!" she sobbed. "Whatever will happen to everyone, will happen to us."

"But try to understand," I started again, "I can't do anything else. Every minute is precious."

"And what will become of us? To whose mercy are you leaving me? Will I ever see you again?" she cried bitterly.

I tried to console her. "I will not run away from you forever. It's for a couple of days, away from the town. As soon as the situation becomes a bit clearer, I'll come back to you."

My older sister, Dina, witness to our conversation, calmed my wife down and consoled her. "Don't worry!" she implored her. "You'll be together with us. Let him run away for the time being. He will surely not abandon you, but will come back to you."

I quickly said good-bye to them and bent down to kiss my 5-year-old daughter. She cried out in pain, putting her hands around my neck. "Daddy," she sobbed, "I don't want to remain alone with Mamma. Don't go away!"

I could not look my child in the eye. "No, Bashele," I cried and implored her. "No. Daddy's not running away. I will soon come back and I'll bring you nice things."

My friend tugged at my sleeve again. I had to leave immediately, afraid to turn my head to meet the sad, tear-swollen eyes of my wife and child. We walked rapidly, and began running through little side streets to the edge of town and the nearby highway leading to the east.

A violent firing of single gunshots could be heard from Grodno. The sun finished its daily course and extinguished itself behind the long day of June 22, 1941. The night stretched out its arms broadly, as if it wanted to console us: "Son of man, find shelter beneath the faithful shadows of my gloom, feel safe in my darkness. I will not betray you. I will cover you and protect you, as a faithful mother protects her child."

Outside Grodno, many people were hiding in the field, crawling on the ground like ants. That morning they'd run away from the city of hell, leaving all their possessions behind to seek shelter in the valleys and ditches of the countryside. The mass of people moved and took shape in the darkness like an anthill. Mothers with their little babies in their arms — hungry, tormented creatures, stumbled over their own feet; others with pale, long, frightened faces asked us, "Is it quiet in the town. Can we go back?"

I hurled an embittered answer at them. "Quiet it may be. But don't go back to town! Run away!" Their confused and wild glances followed us. We speeded our pace and made progress along the highway. After several kilometers, I stopped to catch my breath and turned around to look at the town. In the distance you could see the sky above it was flaming red. Powerful tongues of fire rose into the air. Artillery shells traced bloody semi-circles on the horizon. At every moment, flaming volcanoes flared up at gas stations that were torched. They exploded in a terrible glare, spattering millions of sparks around them, producing light that could be seen scores of kilometers away; then slowly they were extinguished, leaving behind a pale, pink glow in the darkness.

I continued to struggle with my thoughts. "What have I done? I have abandoned my wife and child in the burning town. I am a criminal!" I reproached myself. My child's last words resounded in my ears: "Daddy, don't leave us alone!"

In the dark of night I saw my child's teary eyes, and her tiny, innocent figure stayed with me. As in a vision that would not leave me, I saw her in the flames of the town. It haunted me and drove me back to the town. I swallowed bitter tears and murmured quietly, "Forgive me, my wife and child, when will I see you again? I am the biggest and worst criminal in the world!"

An armored car stopped near us. It was loaded with ammunition that a loyal soldier brought from the border. I dragged myself up on the running board. The soldier did not protest. He complained only that the car was overloaded, the tires were damaged and he was afraid the ammunition might fall into the hands of the Fascists. He pulled a little piece of newspaper from his sleeve, scraped a bit of cheap rolling tobacco out of his pocket and started to smoke. He breathed the smoke in deeply, looked at the burning horizon above the town and stammered out some words.

"What a war! This scoundrel made an agreement with us not long ago. Such heroism! In the middle of the night he attacks with a lot of airplanes. He will be defeated."

A pale moon slipped out from under the clouds and cast a dim glow on the face of this embittered, but not despairing soldier. The highway was full of people and cars — military personnel and civilians, whole groups, couples and single individuals — all rushing eastward. Masses of people of all ages were running on foot into the big, wide world, like frightened lambs chased by wolves. Others carried suitcases, which they later threw away to make their journeys easier. Here and there parents carried little babies like Torah scrolls, after dragging them out of their warm little beds, hoping to disappear with them into the darkness of the night.

With regret I looked at the parents and children. They had only the smallest chance of saving themselves. They did not imagine that Hitler's tanks were moving more quickly, that they would catch up with them.

I took some rolling tobacco from the soldier, had a smoke, and again was overcome by melancholy, worrying about Frumke and Bashele. Deep down in my heart I decided, sitting in the armored car, that however far I would travel, I would still come back, and if I was not able to save myself with them, we would at least die together.

"We'll carry on," called out the driver, who was preoccupied with the tires. The car moved slowly, groaning beneath its heavy load. Sitting there, I felt cold as the biting night air reached into my body and seized my limbs. I was dressed in light summer clothes and wore a raincoat, which offered scant protection against the cold.

Slowly the telegraph poles passed by, one after the other. This created a spark of joy in my soul. That meant we were not fleeing too quickly. The car would not carry us far; I would remain near my wife and child and perhaps tomorrow there would be certain changes at the border and I would be able to go back to them. With such sweet illusions I managed to chase the bitterness from my heart.

By the side of the highway, out in the fields, there were batteries of heavy artillery here and there, with their long necks stretched out like giraffes, looking to the west, completely silent.

"Why are they silent?" I asked myself, "What did people create them for?" They had been the citizens' great hope. Why didn't they start roaring with their amazing strength? They, those iron giants, could still save us. I also quickly gave myself the answer. "Woe to the people whose last hope is in the power of guns!"

The car started to shake, screech and move very slowly. The driver shut off the engine, got out, hurled a curse into the air and informed us resentfully that the tire was completely ruined and the car was riding on its wheel rim. The soldiers rapidly took their rifles out of the cabin, checked their pistols and we all went off on foot to the *shtetl* of Skidel, situated right by the highway, 32 kilometers from Grodno.

It was dawn. Skidel was half a kilometer from the highway, in a small valley. The wooden houses with their tiled and thatched roofs were still standing, as if in deep sleep; it was as though the events around them did not concern them. Yet it turned out that this was last day of life for the comfortable little Jewish *shtetl* of Skidel. A few hours later, the *shtetl*, with its houses of study, its public school, its clubs and all its other little houses, was in flames, burning like rows of candles.

The morning of June 23 broke angrily and full of clouds. Large patches of cloud appeared in the sky, swimming and forming dots in the rising sun. With daybreak, enemy aircraft woke up. Soon the black birds of prey, humming fearfully, appeared between the clouds. To hide from the blinding rays of the rising sun, the planes maneuvered between them. Then they swooped down, and from close behind came powerful booms.

There was no time to stop. We had to go on. Many long-range artillery and anti-aircraft guns were hidden at the side of the road, in a small wood. They were waiting and searching for enemy planes above. The higher-ranking military officers whispered among themselves. From their expressions it was clear the situation was not good and that they were discussing retreat.

Many civilians mingled among the soldiers — the majority of them Jews from Grodno who had no intention of leaving the soldiers, but would march with them. The soldiers did not protest or drive anyone away, either from themselves or from the machines, as they normally would. The mutual affection and trust was strongly felt during the moment of great danger.

"Where are our aircraft?" soldiers asked, bitterly. "Maybe this is one of ours," said a soldier who pointed at an airplane hovering high above the wood. A captain looked through his binoculars for a moment and observed it, and then put his binoculars down and commented bitterly and resignedly: "Yeah, it's one of ours alright, a Fascist one!"

The airplane turned a few circles in the air and swooped down at lightning speed, like a sparrow hawk spotting its prey. It ejected a couple of bombs, almost a hundred meters from where we were. The ground quivered and the bird of prey vanished. Then I realized there was no point in marching with military personnel if I didn't have military training.

I met several people from my work brigade in Grodno. Until that very last day, we were building a shoe factory together. We agreed to go to Minsk and walked at a brisk pace. Our plan was clear: we were to get to Minsk, the capital of White Russia, or perhaps to the old Polish-Soviet border of 1939. We were foolish enough to think that this little piece of Polish territory might be the only issue for Hitler; or that decisive battles would be fought at the eastern border of White Russia, and the Fascists would be defeated. We assumed the Soviet Union would, in all likelihood, fiercely defend its legitimate old frontiers.

How naïve we were, comforting ourselves with foolish illusions. And as the human wish is always father to the thought, we assumed that what we longed for would come true. In the meantime, we unfortunately forgot that the German general staff was also making plans, much more realistic and far-sighted than ours. During the course of a few days, the Fascist armies surrounded the whole of White Russia and we were trapped in the cruel enclave. For us it would be quite a considerable journey to Minsk — about 300 kilometers — and it was almost 200 kilometers to the old border.

We walked energetically, with zest. On the highway, armored cars filled with soldiers moved constantly, as if intoxicated. The soldiers no longer accepted civilians on board. As they retreated, the issues for them were to maintain the cars, keep the ammunition, and escape from chaos to join regular united resistance troops elsewhere. Many armored cars — damaged, burned-out and overturned — were left on the road, along with military equipment — from books and maps to syringes, surgical instruments and bandages. Many motorized cannons were overturned, pushed to the side of the highway. Countless rifles, bullets, grenades and mines were scattered on the ground. All of this was testimony to the panic and the triumph of the devil, as the border regions of the big Soviet Republic disintegrated.

As if to spite us, it had otherwise been a very good year. The fields were laid out, as green as a plush carpet, with their ripe, gleaming vegetables, waiting for the capable hands of the peasant. The golden grain stood high, its ears of plenty bowed down to the ground, waiting for the reaper. The wind mildly rocked the golden ears, whispering to them, as if it wanted to tell them a secret: This year the reaper would not come in time, the sun would dry them up, scatter them, and they carried nature's blessed gift to humanity in vain.

A fresh, pleasant smell of honey rose from the buckwheat fields with their clear white blossoms. They reminded me of the white cloak of snow on the fields of winter. The sun tormented us with its great heat and made our difficult journey even more difficult. Its rays sneaked into our collars and onto our breasts and made our tired bodies even more tired.

It was worse in the open fields because of the Fascist planes. We had to run from them, ingeniously hiding in pits, bushes or between rocks. Like a fatal curse, the planes, appeared suddenly and moved right above the highway and pursued and chased down everyone living. They dropped down low, almost to ground level, and with quick bursts of machine gun fire, poured down a hailstorm of bullets that cut through the highway like razor blades. There was simply nowhere to hide. The murderous machine gun bullets were shelled like peas.

Those were the methods Hitler's bandits used in their war on an unarmed population. Many dead and wounded were left to rot on the highway and in the fields. The wounded who could not move remained where they were. There was no question of getting help, and in agony and pain, they were snuffed out like candles. Others still stirred, and stretched out their hands like drowning men, asking for help. But it did not enter anyone's head to take an interest in the injured, to bandage their wounds or give them a sip of water to drink. Everyone with working legs ran eastward.

In the bushes at the side of the highway, was a badly injured 18-year-old boy dressed in a respectable gray suit. His head was still intact, but his eyes were covered with pus. A big bloody stain was visible on the side of his jacket. His chest heaved ponderously. I threw myself at this lonely unknown boy, who at that moment was so dear and close to me. I asked my friends for a bandage and wanted to dress his wound. But soon a host of planes came buzzing. My friends grabbed me and forcefully dragged me away from the victim. They pulled me deeper into the bushes for protection.

A plane dropped down, turned several circles above the thin bushes, searching and sniffing out the nooks and crannies beneath everyone. Machine gun fire crackled above our heads. Instinctively I fell beneath a shrub, afraid to make any sudden arm or leg movements. The plane flew so low that I could feel the air waves from the propellers on my back. I cast a furtive glance at the hovering plane when it turned another circle, and could clearly see the pilot wearing a helmet. Both his hands were pressing against the automatic machine gun on the side of the plane.

The plane came straight at us. The thought, "I'm finished, this is my grave," flashed through my mind. Reflexively, I huddled my body and tucked my head into my shoulders as much as possible. The machine gun fired a shot above my back, and close to my head, sand exploded in the air. One step closer and the bullets would have been in my head. I got up and asked my friend if I was still alive.

CHAPTER 3

On the Road to Minsk

Dazed, I spent lots of time looking for the injured boy but could not find him anywhere. For many days after that, I saw him in front of my eyes, an unknown boy with a pale face, and could not rest. To avoid meeting any planes head on, we went off the road, continuing our journey through forest clearings, meadows and fields. On our way through the forest we grew more confident. It shielded us faithfully and a provided safe haven.

The forests of White Russia are beautiful. Like well-respected elders, the hundred-year-old fir trees and pine trees stand straight and proud at the sides of the highway. Their dense, green crowns of needles look up at the sky with arrogance. From beneath the bark on healthy trunks, oily resin seeps out in summertime, diffusing the pleasantly fragrant scents of fresh turpentine and tar through the cool forest air.

There was a reason the great Polish poet, Adam Mickiewicz, so ardently longed for these forests after he immigrated to France. He described the glorious, beautiful forests of the Nowogródek and Lida region with love in his work, "*Pan Tadeusz*."

The deep, green moss beneath the trees was like a soft plush sofa, where it was a pleasure to rest one's tired and battered limbs after the long and difficult walk. We sat in the shade of the forest, exhausted, dusty, sweaty, and burned by the sun. We calculated how many kilometers we had walked and how many were still left to go before we reached Minsk. During the course of 24 hours we had covered almost 100 kilometers and were near the town of Lida, the regional capital. We had not eaten anything all day.

When we were constantly chased by planes, we forgot about our hunger. But now, resting in the soft forest moss, we remembered that we had not eaten and that it was about time to eat. My friend took a piece of dusty rye bread out of his side pocket. Luckily, we found a tin plate with a bit of fat on the highway, left behind by soldiers. We filled ourselves up, rested for about an hour and then had the strength to continue.

The sun set in the west and cast sparse sheaves of light obliquely through the thick shade of the forest path. Like a glowing red ball, the sun slowly drew closer to the earth. Little by little it disappeared, leaving a red sea of fire on the western horizon.

We got to our feet to carry on, but the soft moss drew us like a magnet. It was such a pity to leave it. Our tired limbs were begging us to rest another minute longer, just another minute. Our eyelids began to stick shut, our heads felt strangely heavy and drunken from the fresh, intoxicating forest air. Bit by bit, sleep would have overcome us and rocked our tired bodies in its enticing cradle. But the force that drove us from our homes and hurried us on our way took us into its mighty arms once more, and carried us swiftly on our way.

We walked at a vigorous pace along a path that wound through the dense forest, hoping to arrive in Lida in time to catch the last train to Minsk. Little by little, the forest thinned out and from the side-paths, fields, forest clearings and meadows became visible.

A fully loaded three-ton truck slowly passed us by. Someone inside called my name. We ran towards it, hung onto the running board and with effort, heaved ourselves into a great huddle of people. My friend, the pharmacist Epstein, who had been a member of the town council was there and so was Philip Pestrak (then the People's Minister of Arts in White Russia) — the White Russian poet and deputy of the Supreme Soviet Council. He was very friendly and knew me well. He and his wife sat squeezed into a corner holding their newborn twins in their arms.

He cast a glance at me and shook his head, as if to say, "How do you like my bomb?" But this was not the same joyful and lively Pestrak I knew. Silent and gloomy, he sat bent double on a suitcase filled with all his manuscripts and did not speak a word. I looked at him, at his wife and his two children, at his impressive suitcase, and a foolish thought tickled my mind and provoked me to laughter.

"Where are your wife and child?" Epstein asked, as if cutting my naked body with a whip.

"They stayed behind in Grodno," I answered, not having the courage to look him in the eye.

"Very nice!" he threw back at me contemptuously. "Leaving one's wife and child in the flames and running away alone to save one's own skin!"

Every word stung my body like a needle and hit me where it hurt most. I raised my eyes and answered him. "Who knows if we here are the ones who are safe, and besides, I haven't left my wife and child for good. I'll go back for them," I shouted out in pain.

My shouting was enough to convince him not to torment me with his questions. He stood next to me quietly, head hanging down, and did not ask anything else.

Packed full like a barrel of herring, the truck was overloaded. That was why it moved so slowly, its engine groaning. There was no room to turn around and people were crammed together like a bundle of sticks. The crowd was mixed. There were policemen, civil servants, peasants, village elders; engineers and mechanics who had built aerodromes before the war. There were a number of prisoners in shabby working clothes, who had served long prison sentences working at the aerodromes the Soviet authorities were frantically building in the western regions of White Russia and at the borders.

I looked in amazement at the ordinary citizens punished by the government for various crimes. They could stay behind as free people, and yet they were running back to Russia. I asked myself, "Why are they running away?" After all, they were not Jews. I had to work out the reason for myself — even the most ordinary citizens were great patriots who loved their country. Despite the fact that the authorities had punished them, they were obediently going home and did not want to stay behind as "free people" in the enemy's occupied territories.

(I met many of them later. They were wearing gray uniforms, and carried empty knapsacks on their shoulders. They walked intently at a brisk pace, straight ahead. When they answered my question, these defeated people did not say a harsh or bitter word against the authorities. Despite the fact that they were prisoners, these were people with a unique moral code. I began to respect them and changed my opinion of them completely).

Bearing its heavy cargo, the truck labored to move on. The driver stopped a few times, occupied himself with the engine and grumbled angrily. He said too many people were on board and the motor could not work properly. Of course, no one wanted to get off and walk. The road ahead went uphill. The engine started to grind with all its might and the truck climbed halfway up the hill. Then there was something like a snap from the cabin and the truck stopped in its tracks.

The driver got out of the cabin and angrily informed us: "The gearbox has seized. We can't go on!"

We had no choice but to get off and continue on foot. We were about twelve kilometers from Lida, on a road that was dense and woody and the surrounding forest was pitch dark. Here and there a patch of blue sky could be seen through the trees. My eyelids started to close, my head became heavier by the minute and I wanted to have a nap while walking, but my tired body swayed on its exhausted feet and I risked getting clipped by a tree. We decided to rest and take a nap — for an hour at least. The moment I sat down, I fell asleep like one of the dead. It seemed like just a minute later that someone tugged at my sleeve and I got up. We continued. I was angry and cursed I know not whom. My teeth were chattering with cold.

The night hovered over the forest like a dark cloak. On the long, monotonous path through it, various "forest mirages" began to appear in the darkness in front of my weary eyes. It seemed to me as if huge temples, with many round, polished pillars and high oval windows reaching the roof stood just by the side of the path. A strange kind of light shone from the windows, and little by little I wanted to leave the path, to wander into these weird, enchanted palaces. They seemed so close and drew me to them with such force, all I wanted to do was rest my tired and weary bones for a while and fall asleep, to sleep and sleep and sleep.

Why was this sleepiness latching on to me? How did it creep so deep into my bones? I had no real wish to understand why, and meanwhile I dragged my feet along like a bundle of rags. We were not far from Lida. So why this sudden urge to sleep? I tried to encourage myself. Is it such an odd thing if one does not sleep for a couple of nights under normal circumstances? Does one immediately die? Where is it written that a person needs to sleep every night? I reasoned with myself, but yawned with a wide-open mouth. It's not a tragedy, I convinced myself, and with both hands rubbed my eyes hard and tried to keep them open as wide. Perhaps that could be a remedy against drowsiness.

Then I had a bright idea. I remembered that as a boy, I once worked in a warehouse at night, baking *matzah*. When I would wash my face with cold water in the middle of the night, my sleepiness would disappear for a while. But where does one get water in the middle of a forest at night? I soon solved the puzzle. I rubbed my hands in the forest's grass, which was cold and wet with dew and refreshed my face. Sleep, defeated, withdrew for a while, and my eyes were not that sticky and sleepy any more.

It started to get lighter in the east. The trees started to emerge from the dark, to edge their outlines of trunks and branches. Their needles slowly started to turn green again. Bushes that looked like hills or little houses, or that resembled horseback riders by the wayside, became visible. They shook the night off their twigs and their little green leaves glittered with dew. The eastern light crept higher and higher into the sky, wiping the stars away.

Piece by piece, in the distance, in the forest clearings, single farmhouses and whole villages emerged. Peasants' cottages stood in the distance as if they were assembled in one heap, their white tiles looking like shrouds, their thatched roofs hanging down over the windows, like hats pulled down over one's eyes. They appeared in all their bold rustic simplicity. A white lime milestone by the highway showed a black number — 105 kilometers. That meant we were exactly three kilometers away from Lida.

We went into a cottage close to the town. The White Russian peasant living there received us politely and considerately. He gave us several cold boiled potatoes and a glass of milk, and though it was the first time in my life, it was odd to eat for free in a stranger's house. I did not refuse, but naively and shyly said a heartfelt thank you.

I asked the peasant's wife for a needle and a thread so that I could mend a ripped sock. I sat down on the porch, but try as I might I could not get the thread through the little eye. My hands shook and my head drooped heavily, as if it were cast of lead. Finally, with great effort I managed to pull the thin thread through the big needle. I made several stitches in the sock, but then fell asleep in the middle of my work, as if struck dead.

When I woke, it was midday. The sun was right above my head and cast its warm rays into every corner. I did not see my friends and the peasant told me they had gone off to the railway station to look for a train to Minsk.

I was very annoyed to have been left alone without any friends in an unfamiliar place.

I headed in the direction of the station, hoping to meet my friends. Walking through various little side streets, I arrived in town. Lida looked like Grodno. It was destroyed. Everything was burning. Dense pillars of smoke rose to the sky and covered it like a gray curtain. The beautiful buildings on the main street were in ruins. Walls stood crumbled and burned, like tooth stumps in an old man's mouth. Smoke came out of the broken windows. Fire mercilessly burned everything that could burn and the taller buildings threatened to collapse momentarily.

People ran around like intoxicated mice. In the mad confusion, I saw someone carrying a chair with three legs; another carried a broken, tarnished mirror. Someone else had a bundle of rags on his back. It was not properly tied and a tattered boot hung out of it. People ran around without any destination or purpose, intensifying the panic. Now and then a wave of planes roared above our heads, fanning the air with the wings of the Angel of Death, confounding people who were foolishly hiding — one in a garbage dump, another beneath a small tree growing near the pavement. Someone else stood beneath a doorframe, as if to protect himself from the shrapnel of steel-cased bombs.

Unfortunately people forgot that bombs could lift heavy houses, melt big iron beams in broken buildings and leave them hanging like bent little wires, that bombs could rip up the asphalt and pavement, dig up mighty craters and rip open the sewage system and water pipes. But a frightened person who has gone crazy in a bomb attack easily forgets those things and looks for salvation in a wooden dump, like a frightened ostrich in the desert who hides its foolish head in the sand when chased by hunters.

I no longer had my raincoat, my only coat. The previous day, I wrapped it around a wounded soldier who was sitting in the truck with me and was shivering with cold. I decided to look for the soldier. I asked some people running by the way to the military hospital. But they gave me contradictory directions and then disappeared. Finally I reached a two-story brick building. A soldier with a rifle stood at the gate and I explained what I wanted. He looked at me suspiciously and told me to leave immediately. But I stood my ground, and told him that I had only one coat, that I needed it, and that my sole intention had been to help a wounded soldier. I showed him my papers to prove I was not a spy or secret agent.

That made an impression on him, and he explained that he could not let me in, that I had to consult the senior doctor, who should be arriving soon. Soon the senior doctor arrived. He was an older man, a colonel. He listened to my foolish request with a hint of mockery in his eyes, as if saying, "A real catastrophe is taking place, but this one wants his rain coat right now."

Though the colonel asked me to wait for the assistant surgeon on duty, I understood the stupidity of my situation, and went away ashamed. I walked back through the side streets and headed toward the station. I had to avoid the deep craters from the bombs and climbed over fallen telegraph poles in the middle of the road.

Damaged wooden houses stood at the roadside. In one of these houses — its roof ripped open and one of its walls torn down — a man was lying on the porch, dead on his back. He was bloated and white-faced, staring indifferently at the sky. He was stretched out, with his clothes unbuttoned. On his shirt, towards his belly, was a big red spot of dried blood. It seemed that all the members of the household disappeared in the chaos, leaving the victim to his fate.

A bit further on, near a sparse wooden fence surrounding a little orchard, a soldier wearing a greatcoat was lying on his side. One hand supported his head, as if he was in a deep sleep. The fist his head rested on was bloody. He had probably gotten a splinter in his skull. I thought, "You good-natured, innocent soldier, you must be a son of the vast Ukrainian steppes or of the Siberian *taiga*. You surely didn't imagine you'd give up your young 20 years in some godforsaken little back street, under some fence, in an unjust war against you."

"No one will know what became of your bones in this chaos. Today or tomorrow, the earth will cover you up and you will remain unknown to the whole world, as you are unknown to me. Somewhere a mother will be crying until her death, and somewhere, too, a woman will be longing for you, until she marries for the second time and forgets you."

Grim life showed its sharp claws. It was only the third day of the war and I was looking strangely at those who were killed, as if it had to be like that, as if the dead had to lie in the streets, without no one to care for them, without anyone to grieve for them. Death and murder were becoming a natural phenomenon and worming their way into the bone marrow of the living.

Once, in normal times, people would lead a murderer through the town in chains. Everyone would run after him, curious to look at him, to watch his every gesture and movement, trying to look into his face to see whether he was like everyone else. The police would drive away the curious crowds. They would take him to court and call witnesses. Lawyers, prosecutors and newspapers would write whole pages about him and the town would be agitated like a quiet stretch of water into which someone had thrown a stone. In many cases they would lead the murder victim to his eternal rest with great pomp, give speeches at his grave and erect a memorial. But murder was now a normal thing and a dead person had about as much worth as a fallen autumn leaf beneath one's feet. It would not occur to anyone that each corpse was once a living being, truly a whole world in him.

Completely confused, I went to the station and with wandering eyes, looked for my friends. I felt lonely and strange among the unknown frightened people. Bomber squadrons roared constantly overhead, as they swiftly carried their lethal cargo eastward. Bewildered I looked into the blue summer sky. High above, little dots the size of swallows moved. I stood there for a long time, with my head raised, and could not make out whether they were airplanes or birds.

Little by little they glided proudly in the air on outstretched wings, just like planes. But they did not seem to be planes. Their wings flapped from time to time. They were flying like swallows or sparrow hawks. My fevered imagination could not draw a clear conclusion. I lowered my head and went on.

At the train station a deathly silence prevailed. It was abandoned – no people or trains. The big halls in the station were eerily deserted, the doors wide open, the benches empty. The windows of the ticket office were open, but no one was inside. Here and there someone approached, sniffing and looking around, then disappearing. The railway men and station officials vanished.

I realized I was too late to be a passenger and I could forget about a train. A guard, busy at the water pipes, confirmed my assumption and told me the last train to Minsk left the previous evening, completely packed, and that one could not travel any more, because the rails and bridges on the route were damaged. Several locomotives stood on the tracks. One was smoking and steaming, restlessly moving back and forth and every so often letting out a sorrowful whistle.

Here and there, red freight cars were parked on the sidings. A healthy-looking youth dragged a sack of flour from one of them. A soldier ran to him, hit him in the face and shouted, "What are you looting, you scoundrel?" and pulled out his revolver. Instinctively I turned my head away, but no shot was fired. The youth asked the soldier for forgiveness in broken Russian-Polish and made the soldier understand that he had worked all night and was hungry.

As he spoke, he kept repeating, "I'm working."

"And if you are so hungry, do you need a whole sack of flour? Quick, put the sack back into the wagon!" the soldier roared. The youth dragged the sack back into the wagon and vanished.

Finally I met my friends again and instantly forgave them for abandoning me. Epstein paced up and down, worried because the trains had stopped running. He was troubled that Pestrak would have to drag himself and his little babies on foot. Epstein was still looking for the stationmaster, hoping that because Pestrak was a member of the highest Soviet council, we could at least get a track inspector's railcar for him and leave Lida as quickly as possible. Nothing came of those plans and we continued our journey on foot a few hours later.

When we left Lida by the main road, the sun was low in the western sky. It was stiflingly stuffy and smoky in the street. The stench of burned rubber filled the air. The buildings were on fire and through the burned windows that resembled eye sockets in a skull you could see a glimpse of the rooms that once were. Tiled stoves stood precariously perched on broken floors. Iron beds with wired netting stood next to each other, bearing witness to a bedroom that was there just two days earlier.

The iron was scorched and bent from the heat. Twisted iron beams hung miraculously in the air. Under our feet, were black sheets of pockmarked tin roofing, scattered by the blasts. Roof gutters, tiles, bricks, glass, tangles of telephone lines and electric wires, overturned poles and pieces of wall were heaped in the middle of the road, so that we needed to climb over them. Further out of town, bare stoves and chimneys of burned-down wooden houses still stood. They looked at the sky with trepidation, as if waiting for the wind to finish tearing them down. Around the solitary chimneys, large embers were strewn around, along with coal, metal objects and kitchen utensils, hinges, and other things that fire had not consumed.

We hurried, wanting to escape this painful panorama as soon as possible. The road led to Lipniszki, a small town, 22 kilometers from Lida. We hoped to get there in a few hours' time, as dusk fell.

Disturbing news reached us from all sides. The Germans were very close. Refugees told us that they had seen them and had difficulty escaping. There were roaring noises from all sides. In the forest, the field artillery pounded incessantly. Dull double beats — thud-thud — like balls bouncing on a sports field, could be heard from all directions. The accompaniment of machine-gun fire and single gunshots hastened us on our way.

The plump Polish peasants stood at the doors of their village cottages, on the porches, at the fences and gates of their yards, looking angrily at us, keeping a grim silence. In their eyes there burned a little fire of pleasure and revenge. The old order was being overthrown, the powers that be were leaving and soon a new Messiah would be born to save them.

The smarter, more cunning peasants did not sit around with their arms folded and did not sleep through the golden opportunity to accumulate riches. They grabbed the discarded luggage that unfortunate refugees threw to the sides of the road to lighten their load. They looted abandoned baggage carts that stood on the highway, and were not ashamed to ask the unfortunate, hungry refugees for gold and jewelry in exchange for a glass of milk, a few potatoes or a piece of bread.

The boldest of them, whose hearts were ill-disposed towards the Soviet powers, picked up the weapons thrown away by deserters and went off into the dense forest, firing bullets over the heads of the retreating military personnel, increasing the panic. The soldiers could not understand these people at all. Deeply hurt and insulted, they angrily cried: "This is the thanks we get for chasing away the aristocrats?"

And in saying this, they would throw in a curse, "You rotten slaves of dogs." With fury, the soldiers hurled themselves on the ground and shot their machine guns blindly into the forest, in the direction of the previously heard shots. At the same time, they were careful not to shoot at the windows of any Polish peasant's house.

I admired the steely forbearance of these simple soldiers, who did not hold the community at large responsible for an individual's behavior — as the majority of soldiers in other armies did in moments of chaos, when they would kill innocent people for the sins of others. "One day they'll cry in memory of us and beat their breasts," the soldiers said bitterly, and got up, cleaned the dust off their uniforms and moved on.

I went to a well in a Polish peasant's yard to drink some water. There was a historical picture on display in the house window and beneath the picture there was the inscription, "The Last Days of Stefan Czarniecki."[1] The picture showed the hetman of Poland, Czarniecki, sitting sadly, with dead soldiers and horses lying at his feet, with broken weapons of war. I quickly understood who this dark-souled peasant referred to. "You'll quickly see your mistake," I grumbled to myself. "Don't think, you foolish peasant, that you will suck on honey under the new Messiah!"

The roaring heavy artillery sounded muffled when it echoed through the forest. Underfoot were splinters of steel. Here and there in the forest, a farmhouse still stood, burning with hellish flames. The flames devoured the wooden walls voraciously, making them sound like the crack of the small bones of a sheep in the jaws of a wolf. The owners hid in the forest, watching in agony, as years of labor went up in smoke.

Slowly the night started to draw in. The sun disappeared somewhere beneath the forest. The air became cooler and a dense fog silently covered the tree-tops. As we traveled, now and then, we heard fresh news about small towns and crossroads being occupied, highways cut off by gangs and the landing of enemy paratroopers.

This news induced an eerie apathy, the realization that all our running and striving was a waste of time. Either way, we were like mice near a trap and sooner or later, we would be caught. But some force pushed us further and further on, as if a hand with a whip was lashing us from behind: "Run faster; don't look back, just run!"

Above the forest, in the distance, rockets rose up into the sky in a blue arc and fell like shooting stars. The rumors were true: we were breathing en-

---

1 Stefan Czarniecki or Stefan Łodzia de Czarnca Czarniecki (1599-February 16, 1665) was a Polish-Lithuanian Commonwealth general and nobleman. He was Field Hetman of the Crown of the Polish Kingdom. He was a military commander, and regarded as Polish national hero. His status in Polish history is acknowledged by a mention of his name in the Polish national anthem.

emy air. We arrived on the outskirts of Lipniszki after dark and came across several farmhouses, with their thatched roofs and small windows, from which the light of the peasants' kerosene lamps was barely visible. Shaggy dogs met us with vile barking, as if we were insignificant, uninvited visitors. With fence poles and stones we showed the dogs that we were not pleased to see them either, and very kindly, as it should be, thanked them for their dog's welcome.

Lipniszki appeared under our noses, with its little market streets and old wooden whitewashed farmhouses. In the marketplace there was buzzing like a beehive around the few government shops. A jingling of little iron lamps, a groaning of shutters and the sound of breaking glass filled the twilight.

Peasants with hot, angry red faces worked with all their might to break open the door of the liquor store, to get every last drop of booze out. They crept through the shattered window like demons, dragging out bottles of liquor and drank to each other's health straight from the bottle, right on the spot. Empty bottles were scattered on the market square and drunken peasants shakily crept through the broken window again, laughing wildly and joking coarsely, aimlessly cursing no one in particular.

To our astonishment, we did not find any of the town's Jews at this "noble" task. A very old man crept by, bent double, and in a shaky voice pointed to a Jewish house hardly distinguishable from a peasant's farmhouse. We opened the door with a warm "good evening" and found ourselves in a big, simple furnished room with a big square table in the center, where Jewish neighbors, young and old, sat in disarray.

Along the whitewashed walls were long benches where dusty and bewildered wayfarers sat. On the table was half a loaf of rye bread, half a bowl of congealed cold grits, empty tea-glasses and a few pieces of sugar on a little saucer. A kerosene lamp with a shade was suspended from a beam above the table, casting feeble light. The walls were hung with large portraits of old people, grandmothers in wigs and grandfathers in skullcaps.

In a corner above a chest of drawers hung a large portrait of a rabbi, probably the Rav of Słonim or the Vilna Gaon. Their frozen expressions looked indifferently upon the crowd. Smaller pictures showed Czar Nicholas's soldiers wearing round caps. The soldiers, with their long, twisted moustaches, looked like the true Russians of long ago. In another picture, images of the recent past, young men, soldiers of the former Polish army, small-town boys and girls, sat next to one another like starchy little statues, quite prim and proper, on a grassy field and a bench under a tree. A picture of the Western Wall in the Holy Land, not exactly painted by a careful hand, hung in the opposite corner. It gave the impression of a ruin of stones, over and around which fir trees grew.

In the center of the wall was a gaudily painted picture on thick paper — apparently by an amateur from the household — commemorating the anniversary of someone's death. At the sides one could see two black candles, with the tablets of the Ten Commandments above them and the mark of Cain beneath them, with the deceased's middle name and the date of his death below. This was a testament that for generations, a comfortable, quiet, folkish small-town Jewish life had prevailed here.

There was an air of grief, as if people were still sitting on the floor in mourning for the deceased. They were not speaking normally — when everyone talked at once, one louder than the other. In fact, they were not talking at all. They were sitting hunched-up, with their heads bowed, and from time to time someone tossed out a measured word.

The broken and depressed homeowners beseeched us to eat, looked at us and the way we were dressed and wiped away a tear. A woman from Grodno, also a traveler passing through, looked into my face, asked what my name was. When I answered, she burst into spasmodic sobbing. I didn't recognize her, and she was wailing so openly over my bitter fate. I moved into the shadows, and with my dusty hand, wiped my own wet eyes.

We did not have to be asked to eat twice. We cleaned our hands, sat down at the table and ate fresh rye bread with a hearty appetite, washing it down with fresh, still-warm milk.

Desperate questions were asked, mainly by the women: "What shall we do? Where shall we run with our little children? How can we leave behind our houses and our cows and all our property?"

"They'll probably be here soon, those devils!" warned another woman from a corner. An older Jew spoke slowly: "We don't need to worry. God is our father. He'll save us from this misfortune, too. I've survived four wars, lived through pogroms. And we'll get rid of this Haman as well! We need to have trust and faith in the One who lives forever!" he comforted us.

"It's alright for this grandfather. He's got a will of iron," said a young boy with ridicule. "But just listen to what people are telling us, grandfather, about what they do to the Jews! You also heard today, what that young man from Warsaw told us, how they force the Jews to lick the muddy wheels of their cars with their tongues, how they order the Jews to lie down in the mud and they walk over them as if they were bridges, how they brand Jews with swastikas, how they whip them to death! And you're talking about miracle!" Out of bitterness, the boy stopped himself short.

"It's still not like they make it out," the old man was contending. "Who cares what they tell us. What do I know? The whole world is not lost, blood is not water, and they will surely not kill a whole community of Jews, God forbid! It's not so bad. The One who is above will help us!" the old man concluded reverently.

The unknown yet familiar woman wept quietly, a sad accompaniment to a melancholy song.

I have always loved the little Jewish shtetl — its simplicity, its folk culture and its good-hearted people, settled for generations in their farmhouses. For the most part they were simple folk, half peasants, with their little plots of land and their cows, living from the labor of their own hands. They were also the village tailors, village shoemakers and artisans who worked for the non-Jewish peasants; they were poor peddlers who wandered all week to the nearby villages, wearing coarse peasant coats, trading "fancy" goods for flax and pig's hair. On Fridays, they rode their lively horses home to their wives and children to celebrate the Sabbath.

For generations the shtetl lived more or less comfortably with its community leaders, cultural organizers and clerics, slumbering between different social epochs. Jewish stock was deeply rooted in the small *shtetls*, where the people spoke the language of Sholem Aleichem and Mendele Mocher Sforim, filling the shtetl with their various characters. Now this ancient race was wavering and suffering and about to collapse.

"Let's keep moving," someone said. Soon we said friendly good-byes to those good people. They wept over us, gave us bread for the journey and hoped to see us alive and well in better times. We left and followed the road that led to Iwje — another small Jewish shtetl, 15 kilometers from Lipniszki. With full bellies and a bit of rest, we energetically marched ahead in the cool night air. Our group had become significantly smaller. Some stayed in Lipniszki to spend the night, feeling that we were too late anyway, and therefore did not consider it worthwhile to strain their feet in vain. They were too ashamed to reveal their doubts about our goal.

We still had a considerable journey ahead of us to get to the old 1939 Soviet border. We were sustained by the thought that great events would take place at the border to transform or ease our situation. It was no surprise that we were drawn to cross the frontier as soon as possible.

Lots of disorganized military personnel from different units marched energetically along the highway. They were exhausted and looked gloomy. The terrifying sight of so many burned-out cars and tractors on the road unnerved us. A soldier, on guard at a bridge, stopped us, asked for our documents, checked them and allowed us to continue. He also told us the enemy was not far away and that we had to be careful — he was shooting spies and subversives who increased the panic by shooting at Soviet officers and signaling to enemy aircraft.

A soldier walking next to me could not understand why Polish peasants from Western White Russia were such nationalists that they shot at Red Army soldiers and suddenly smiled so broadly at Hitler. I tried to explain the mystery to him: perhaps the Polish farmer disliked the *kolkhoz* (the farming collectives).

"Yes," the soldier answered with sarcasm, "if one has ten or fifteen acres of land, maybe five cows and several servants, one might well dislike the *kolkhoz*."

In those days the contrast between the rich Polish farmers and poor peasants who understood the enemy on the one hand and the Soviets on the other, was more noticeable. The Polish burghers, who were waiting for the Soviets to retreat, sharpened their teeth on the Jewish poor, and considered them allies of the Soviet Union.

Promoting antisemitsim was unnecessary, since in recent years the official "OZON" party in the Polish national government conducted an intense antisemitic propaganda campaign, imitating the inflammatory propaganda against the Jews in Germany in all its details. From time to time they instigated local pogroms and had obvious links to Goebbels' propaganda ministry in Berlin. The Jewish masses were caught between these allies as between hammer and anvil.

As we marched, we were plagued by the dense dust hanging like a fog above the bullet-riddled highway. It settled on our faces in a thick layer, turned our heads white, and glued itself to our sweaty bodies, covering us with an unusual mud. It crept into our eyes, throats and noses. The dust was stubbornly stuck in our nostrils, stopping up our noses like corks, and we swallowed the dusty air. The sand gritted our teeth. Now and again we spat the mud out to allow us to breathe normally. Inevitably, it made it difficult to move quickly.

I struggled and tried to free my airways. I did it so clumsily that a stream of blood welled up from my nose and soiled my face, my hands, my shirt and even my trousers. My body was tired and my heart was pumping hard. The hot blood streamed forcefully out of my nose and didn't stop.

I lay down on my back and held my head in different positions without success. My faithful friends stood over me, worried. Each offered a different piece of advice, but nothing helped. I stopped up my nose with a piece of linen from my shirt and swallowed the blood. There was not even mouthful of cold water to be had. It was night in the dark forest and no one knew where to find a village or cottage.

"Go," I said to my friends, "don't stay with me. It's a waste of time. Wait for me in the shtetl. I'll come a bit later, when I get better." In the darkness a rustling noise could be heard and two empty trucks slowly passed us by. I dragged myself up from the ground and ran toward the trucks. I caught up with them, grabbed one of the high sideboards and struggled to haul myself in. A soldier sitting in the truck told me to leave the vehicle alone and not jump in.

"Let me in and I'll explain to you!" I shouted to him and crawled in, stretching out on the floor of the truck. The soldier bent down, looked at my bloody face and defended himself: "You have to understand. We're going to a restricted area. I must not take any civilians there. I will be punished by the commander."

I held my bloody nose with one hand and with the other dragged my passport out of my pocket. He grumbled in the darkness: "I don't need your passport. I see you're injured and that's good enough for me. But we don't have any medical facilities there. We won't be able to help you at all. I don't want to get another telling-off from the commander for taking a civilian to a secret place," he concluded and sat down on a gasoline drum, silent.

Judging by how long it took us to pass the telegraph poles at the side of the highway, I realized that we were driving slowly. I was on my back, looking at the starry deep blue sky and swallowing the blood in my throat. After half an hour's drive, the vehicle left the highway. The telegraph poles disappeared as we drove a short distance down a side road in the forest. Then the vehicle stopped.

Between the trees, the long throats of long-range defense artillery protruded. The soldier explained to a superior that a civilian covered in blood crawled into the truck. The commander jumped into the truck, eyed me suspiciously, asked for my passport, glanced at it and said in a commanding tone: "Get off the truck. We don't have medical aid here. Get out of here; this is a restricted area."

I had no choice. I had to leave the truck. A soldier, on duty at the cannons, looked at my bloody face, took a pile of cigarettes out of his pocket, pressed them into my hand and said: "You have to get away from here! Go out to the highway. Lie down on your side in the cold grass and smoke. You'll feel better."

I followed the soldier's advice, and the bleeding finally stopped. I stayed at the side of the highway for quite some time, hoping to meet my friends again. I soon realized that I probably traveled about 10 kilometers by truck and that they would not arrive all that quickly. I set off on the dark forest path. Dawn broke. The eastern sky reddened before sunrise and enemy planes once again roared in the bright early morning.

There was an empty truck on the right side of the highway. I opened it and pulled down its left sideboard. Then I gathered some fir-tree branches, threw them in the back, pulled myself on board and lay down on my side facing the highway. I hoped my friends would pass by soon, see me, wake me up and we would continue. I covered myself up to my head with the branches, hoping to camouflage myself from the planes that constantly searched and lurked in the sky. Tired and weak from loss of blood, I fell asleep immediately.

Soon I felt someone busying himself with me, turning me from side to side. I barely opened one eye and saw a peasant standing with his shoulder turned towards my face, going through my pockets thoroughly. In a flash I realized what was happening and with all my strength, hit him in the face. The thieving peasant must have been scared to death. He crossed himself and stuttered in Polish that he thought I was dead, and wanted to give me a decent burial.

"Because it is a great sin," he craftily tried to convince me, "if a living person sees someone who's got killed and he doesn't bury him."

"Don't look to do a good deed for the dead," I answered the cunning robber. "It would be better not to inconvenience yourself, and give the hungry passer-by some bread to eat and the thirsty a drink of water. That would be a finer good deed for you."

Only later did I learn my friends had passed by and tried to wake me up, but I was fast asleep. They apparently noticed my bloodied shirt and concluded I was dead. They left me and spread the rumor that they had seen me — dead — on the road.

I marched off at a rapid pace, because I wanted to reach Iwje quickly. The sun, though still low in the sky, lent some warmth to the sharp early morning. My mouth was dry and sickly after the fair portion of blood I swallowed. I was very thirsty. There was a neatly-kept peasant's house with a tin roof, wide windows and a carved porch on the side of the road. (The householder was a Polish colonist). I entered and could feel the air of peasant self-satisfaction and affluence.

The peasant's wife was busy cooking breakfast at the stove and the peasant, a healthy-looking fellow with a red face, was chopping wood. I greeted them with a warm "good morning" and asked, "Maybe you could spare a glass of milk. I'm tired and thirsty from my journey. Or perhaps you can give me just a bite to eat. I don't expect it for free. I can pay you, as much as you would want." The peasant's wife said, as if talking to the chimney, "We don't have anything." The peasant drew himself up, cast a frosty glance at me and answered: "We don't have anything, no milk and no bread, and we don't need your money."

He emphasized these last two words "your money." In the middle of the room was an uncovered milk churn, still foaming, apparently with milk fresh from the cow. On the opposite wall hung a big, colorful picture of the Holy Virgin with the son of God in her arms. I looked hard at Jesus' face to see if he turned red from shame over what his love of humanity had come to.

The peasant noticed my glance at the picture and started stammering. "You must understand the milk belongs to our neighbor. If you had something to give in exchange, some nice towel or something, I would have got some milk for you." With bitterness I looked at the peasant's well-fed face, from which stupid and senseless hostility poured out. My hands were itching, and in the heat of the moment I would gladly have hit him in face and shouted into his ears loud enough for the whole village to hear: "You miserable, dark soul of a peasant, we are innocent!!!"

Angrily I shut the door behind me, went out into the courtyard and drank my fill of cold water from the well. My thirst disappeared instantly and my tongue became soft and supple again. I marched enthusiastically toward Iwje. In the distance I could see the cross of the town's church.

I entered a small town on the highway from Lipniszki to Iwje, and though it was still very early morning, there was dew on the little leaves in the town's small orchards that caught the rays of the rising sun and dissolved them into the glinting colors of the rainbow. There was also a great bustle and commotion in the narrow streets. Agitated and very absorbed, I could see the gloomy faces of the town's Jews, young and old, as they rushed from one neighbor to the other. Some were empty-handed, others had bags or bundles on their shoulders. They were probably looking for advice, to ask a wise neighbor for his opinion at such a critical moment.

One older Jew was barely able to carry his large bundle of bedding. It was wrapped in a red, padded blanket. Bent double, the old man stumbled over his own feet. Apparently he was trying to run as quickly as the young men with their bundles. But it was too much for him. He staggered like a drunk and the bundle laid him low without mercy. Then apparently he forgot something and went back. The early morning breeze played with his gray beard. He stumbled over his old feet, going back the same way he came, sweaty, out of breath. He stopped right next to me, breathing as heavily as a blacksmith's bellows. His eyes beneath his dense eyebrows were looking down at the ground, as if he was looking for something there.

"Let's see about your bundle, uncle. I'll help you!" I said to him.

"I forgot something else," he said, as if talking to himself, and entered a little house nearby that stood with its door open. I followed the old man into the house. He looked at me, did not ask me anything, and with all his strength pushed an old, worn-out garment into the bundle. No one was in the little house except the two of us. It stood there like an abandoned nest. A simple bare table stood in the middle of the room. An uncovered bare iron bed with a wire base stood against the wall, and there were a few rough stools and a rickety chair. Above the table a lamp with a glass lampshade surrounded by little glass holders with glass beads hung on a wire — all fly-specked.

"What use is this rag to you?" I asked. "That bundle is too much for your strength ," I said.

"They'll be here soon. They're not far as it is," he grumbled in despair, as if speaking out of a barrel. He raised his melancholy eyes, as if he had only just noticed me, looked for a moment at my dusty appearance and probably realized that I was just passing through. Trembling like a *lulav* (a palm frond used on the Sukkot holiday), he said to me: "Have mercy! Run away from here! As fast as you can! They'll soon occupy the town. They're close, a few versts[2] from here."

"Where are you running to, uncle?" I asked. He thought for a while and then stammered, "How do I know where to run? One runs into the grave." And with all his strength he packed his garment into the sack. "My wife and children have run away in the night, to some non-Jewish acquaintances in the villages, and I've stayed to look after our house. I'm carrying my things to my non-Jewish neighbors to hide here in the *shtetl*. They won't keep them after all and they'll give them back to me later on," the old man said defensively, saving me from asking the question. I took his sack on my shoulders and again he grumbled, "Run away! Run away, as quickly as you can! They'll soon be here."

I sat down on a chair in the middle of the empty room, and the old man's last words resounded in my ears like a dark prophecy: Where should one run? One runs into the grave.

Maybe the old man is right, I thought, maybe it is a waste of time to run and suffer for no reason, and maybe my friends were not so wrong to go back home.

Maybe I should have gone back to Frumke and Bashele and not wandered from home in unfamiliar territory. Who knows where my feet will lead me, where I will catch a bullet and under which bush I will die. Who will remember me and cry a tear for me? None of my nearest and dearest will know where my bones are, and my name won't even be written on my grave marker. Some good-hearted Jewish or non-Jewish gravedigger might scrawl on a simple board: "An unknown dead man of about 30 rests here."

If he still has energy, he might add the date and, in all probability, a very imminent date, because that seemed the most realistic prospect. It would be just punishment for deceiving my wife and child, abandoning them and running away to save my own skin.

Such gloomy, pessimistic thoughts took hold of me in the empty little house in Iwje.

I shook myself, as if awakening from a somber dream, got up and mur-

2 A verst is an old Russian measure equivalent to a little bit more than a kilometer.

mured to myself, "Never! I'm not running away from my wife and child! I'll come back to them for sure. I'll come back!" And my wholesome thought also prompted me to move. "Forward, my friend! Forward, because for the time being there's no way back. The plague has been spreading behind your back and the watchful eyes of brown snakes are lying in wait for Jewish blood. Forward, my friend! Forward! If there's a chance to go back, I'll let you know."

There was a water mill on a little bridge over the stream, just at the edge of the *shtetl*. Next to it stood the miller, a Jew of about 40, looking anxiously into the dark water. His eyes cast down, as if he noticed something in the water. It flowed over the turbine and turned it slowly, singing a melancholy song of "*tlap-tlap*."

The water rushed down, pressing against the green, moldy sluice and moving with determination across the tilted wooden floor into the river. Seeing the clear, lively stream, I wanted to throw off my dusty clothes and refresh my tired body in the pleasant water. But the old man's words came into my mind: "Run away as quickly as possible. They're close!"

Indeed there was no point in taking a bath right now. I could cover about ten kilometers in the time it would take to bathe.

"Tell me, brother," I interrupted the miller's thoughts. "How many kilometers to get from here to Bakszty and is this the right way?"

The miller gave me a sad look and replied gloomily. "It's 28 kilometers to Bakszty. And the path you are on will take you there." He looked down at the river again, motionless. This man intrigued me, with his dry answers and his stiff posture. I stood next to him for a while, as if I were tied there, holding on to the handrail of the bridge, looking at him furtively, and pretending to look into the water.

I felt very drawn to this man and wanted to get a few words out of him.

"Tell me, brother," I turned towards him, "They say in your *shtetl* that the Germans are very close, and you are standing here quietly, as if it were just a usual day, looking into the water. Why haven't you run away until now? Doesn't it matter to you?"

He gave me a bitter look, as if I disturbed his slumber, and answered: "What do you mean, running? Where should I run with my wife and children? And to whom should I leave the mill? Don't you know that the mill has provided me with bread for 15 years? Do you mean I should abandon the mill and go around the wide world, begging for my bread?"

"But life is more precious," I said.

"I've worked out all kinds of plans during these past few days and reckoned up, measured and weighed up everything all over again and I don't even have the strength to think any more. My brain is about to dry up. And then again, am I so blessed in the eyes of God? Whatever will happen to all the Jews will happen to me. Anyway, one doesn't die twice!" he concluded.

"You're almost right," I murmured, said good-bye and went to Bakszty.

As swiftly as arrows, my companions and I headed to Bakszty. In the dense Naliboki forests there was constant roaring and the ground trembled from the ceaseless artillery fire that hit the whole region continuously and persistently. The dense White Russian forest, where more than ten thousand partisans and thousands of Jews would later find shelter, was baying in the strident language of war.

The centuries-old silence of that place never heard such powerful artillery bombardment. The enemy armies had a tough nut to crack getting through the dense, wildly overgrown paths. Wherever one went, there were camouflaged artillery and tanks, continuously exchanging fire with the enemy.

Enemy aircraft could not do very much in the dense greenery and sea of trees. Without an exact target beneath them, the German planes flew low above the forest, searching, sniffing out and lying in wait for the Soviet military units, which fired at their attackers haphazardly. Without specific targets, the enemy planes relentlessly hurled heavy bombs into the forest, gouging deep pits in the dense canopy, tearing out trees and their roots and shattering old forest giants into woodchips.

The dense forest was a natural fortress for us. The shrapnel lodged in the trees and did not have much effect on us, so we walked boldly ahead and did not really count kilometers. Every ten kilometers or so, we rested for ten minutes. We found a Soviet colonel with several officers, at a crossroads, observing something in the distance. I walked up and asked whether it was safe to walk in the direction we were going and whether we would fall into the hands of the enemy.

He thought for a moment and answered, "I can't tell you for sure. But it's a fact that these bandits are very close. My advice for you, little doves, is to take the road that leads to Baranowicze. For the time being the road is still safe and I guess that you'll get there in peace."

We had no desire to put in another few dozen kilometers' foot-slogging but we decided to go ahead, come what may, as long as we got to the border as quickly as possible.

Two kilometers from Bakszty, a little out of the way, was the Jewish settlement Berezina. There were a dozen or more beautiful houses and several *minyanim* of Jews had lived there for generations as farmers and cattle breeders. The spacious houses, the big barns and cowsheds testified that the inhabitants were hard working and wealthy people.

When we approached the little village, a young Jewish man, riding a beautiful, strong horse, greeted us like a true brother and invited us like old acquaintances to get some rest and eat something in the settlement. I liked the Jewish rider's lively smiling face, where there was no trace of worry or sadness despite dangerous times. He sat proud and free on his restless horse, laughed at us like a true brother, pulled the reins and repeated again and again: "Come, come to us. You'll get a bit of rest, and at the same time you'll see how Jewish farmers live."

We shook hands cordially, my melancholy disappeared somehow, and we entered one of the houses — the rabbi's house. The rabbi, a man of about 50, dressed in a fine, graceful and imposing way, with the trimmed beard of a *Misnaged*, an opponent of Hasidism, sat at the head of the table and diligently read the Ethics of the Fathers out aloud (as it was *Shabbes*.)

When he saw us, he greeted us with a warm handshake, gestured to us to sit down and returned to his recital. In the room there was an air of *Shabbes*. The table was covered with a beautiful floral cloth, on which stood two tall, elegant nickel candlesticks. The walls were decorated with green wallpaper, and several large pictures of rabbis in bronze frames hung on the walls, as well as a fine embroidery of the Western Wall. Near one wall there was a beautiful, veneered cupboard with a centered mirror, and against the opposite wall stood a few gleaming arch-backed chairs. An old-fashioned, yet beautiful lamp hung from the ceiling and the windows were hung with clean tulle curtains. The floor was painted red and shone like a mirror. I could hardly believe that this was a rabbi's room and all the more so in a little village.

I looked into the mirror unintentionally and hardly recognized myself. My clothes were white with dust from the journey, my face burned black by the sun, my neck dirty from the grime, my hair hanging tousled from my head, gray from the sand and dust that had collected in it during the journey.

Then I realized I was in the rabbi's house without a head covering. I signaled to my friends and we went out on tiptoe, not wanting to disturb the rabbi's service. We crossed the threshold and went into another Jewish home. Here, too, we were welcomed and received with open arms. The village Jews received us heartily, greeted us with a cheerful "Shalom-Aleichem" and with their hard callused palms, warmly pressed our hands.

The Jewish mothers in the village clasped us to their bosoms, as if we were their own children. They looked at us and wiped their eyes. Some Jewish village girls, shy, charming ones, brought us soap and clear, white towels. They led us to the well and with their skillful countrywomen's hands quickly drew water, poured it for us, as obliging sisters would, and helped us wash ourselves clean.

After that, they laid the table for us, wholeheartedly and with open hands, filling it with the village's plenty. The young village boys prepared places for us to sleep in the fragrant hay of the big barn. Every nook of the house evidenced the fullness and plenty of peaceful village life that lasted for generations. And though the forest outside was roaring and the wave of destruction was approaching, among the Jews here there was a sense of chaos and panic. These Jewish farmers sat there strong as oak trees, deeply rooted in their portion of land, as if the gathering storm was no concern of theirs.

What did people in this oasis think? I could not imagine. Did they think that the storm would not affect them? Did they believe that, with their roots firmly in the ground, they would survive this crisis as well? Either way, it was good to breathe freely for a couple of hours in their quiet, comfortable setting. The blight of panic faded away and we truly felt as if we were in an oasis, somewhere amid desert storms.

"Come and see how Jewish farmers live, look at our wealth and hard work!" the householder said after the meal. I went outside with him. He opened a big cowshed not far from his house and we went inside. In the clean, tidy shed there were six cows without halters chewing cud and looking at us stupidly. The fur shone on their plump, well-fed bodies. With their thick necks and fattened flanks, the cows stood engrossed in their labors. It was obvious that a good, skillful farmer was looking after them.

"As you can see, this is the fruit of my labor — the best cows in the whole region!" the householder boasted. "I'm not short of butter, cheese or milk, thank God! In addition to this, there are about a hundred chickens and two horses. One horse you've seen, of course, along the way. My son went out to meet all the refugees and invite everyone to our house to get some rest. And apart from this, we've got about eight acres of our own land. We're not lacking even in hen's teeth. We bake *hallah* from our own wheat."

I could not understand the cool, complacent attitude of this Jewish farmer at all. In such times, when people's very footsteps were burning holes in the ground, he spoke lightly about his goods. I could not comprehend or accept this at all.

"What are you planning to do next?" I asked casually.

"I'm not planning anything," he answered dryly. "We are simple country folk and don't understand politics. We've been established here for generations and every inch of every field is saturated with our sweat. We can't run anywhere. We won't abandon the labors of many generations. We can't tuck our wealth into our pockets and run off. All our riches are in our cowsheds and barns and in our fields. We don't really want to dwell on it too much either. Whatever happens to all the Jews, will happen to us."

I could not ask this Jew any more pointless questions, and realized the significance of his answer. Standing in the shed next to the cows and talking to this Jewish farmer, I really began to understand why there was no hysterical panic in this little Jewish village.

It was the not-so-smart peasant logic, which has no grasp of abnormal phenomena and does not understand irregularities, which imagines today to be like yesterday and tomorrow like today. It cannot think any other way and for him the essential thing was his attachment to his land.

Either way, I did not want to argue with this good-hearted Jewish farmer any more or rub salt into his wounds. Night fell and a thick fog descended slowly upon the dense woodlands surrounding the little Jewish village. The artillery with its double booms did not stop roaring in the forests round about. On the contrary, it sounded stronger and nearer. Many tired Jewish travelers were in the barn, some snoring heavily in the soft, fragrant hay while others made plans for the next day.

We were not far from the border — about 40 kilometers. The nearest border town was Vołma. In order to get there, we had to go through the town of Iwieniec, between Bakszty and Vołma. My traveling companion, Berl Israelske, one of my school friends and with whom I survived the whole hellish journey from Grodno to Bakszty, would not let me rest and constantly jumped up from his spot and begged me to continue the journey immediately. Time was precious, he argued. During the night we could cover a fair bit of road. But I was against it, if only because of the persistent rumor that detachments of German paratroopers were lying in wait in the forests and mercilessly killing the Jews they caught on the road.

"Come," he begged me, "exactly because it's night, that's the best time. We'll steal through the dangerous stretch of road and at dawn we'll be at the border." I stuck firmly to my own point of view and went to sleep. He turned away from me angrily and soon disappeared in the dark of the night. I never heard from him again. It is possible he was killed by a German bullet that night, or by Polish forest bandits, who were common in that region and who, in those terrible days, helped the Germans with their "noble work" - killing and robbing Jewish travelers.

Polish peasants told about seeing the Germans and talking to them, that the Germans had given them cigarettes and even smiled at them. These crafty Polish peasants would present these fairy tales in lavish detail while describing how neatly the Germans were dressed and how red and well fed their faces were. In broken Russian they would go over it again for the Soviet soldiers on retreat, tired, hungry and in disarray like ruminating cows. That was a cunning kind of moral subterfuge, a hint to the soldiers that there was no reason to run away; that the devil was absolutely not as black as he had been painted.

The next morning we said good-bye to the kind-hearted Jewish farmers of Berezina. They gave us food for the journey, clasped our hands and wished us a successful journey and hoped we would meet again alive and well! God alone knew if this wish was ever going to be fulfilled.

I glanced one last time at the little Jewish village and whispered quietly: "A miracle, only a miracle can save us." At that moment I remembered the words of one of Shimon Frug's poems.[3]

> The sound of thunder can be heard from afar,
> The lightning flash burns in our eyes.
> Oh, God, have mercy on the poor,
> Save us from the dark and stormy skies!

Yes, only God and a miracle could still save us.

---

3   Shimon Frug was a Russian Yiddish poet (1860–1916).

CHAPTER 4

Russian Soldiers

We took a shortcut through the densely-wooded Naliboki Forest on a main path. Every ten or fifteen kilometers there were poor little White Russian villages along the road. Hunchbacked cottages with small windows, like narrowed Chinese eyes, looked at us gloomily. Thatched roofs overgrown with green moss testified that poor peasants lived there in penury. Thirsty, we threw ourselves at half-collapsed, stagnant wells, drawing some water with wooden buckets and cheerfully drank cold water that tasted of mud and mildew. Here and there some poor peasants invited us to their cottages and offered us a few potatoes or a handful of groats, helped us count the kilometers and showed us the right way.

The White Russian peasants of that region behaved very well toward us in those terrible days. It is not clear whether this was because they themselves were oppressed by the Polish noblemen and colonizers for so many years and therefore saw the Soviet Union as their liberator. Perhaps it was because the sword of Damocles — the threat of being ruled by Nazi overlords — was hanging over their heads. Either way, in their sympathy for us, their bewilderment and dread about their own future could clearly be seen.

One White Russian peasant poured milk for us from a clay jug. He cried and said: "My son went off to war with the Red Army. God alone knows if he's still alive. Drink, little doves. You are also lonely, after all, and are being chased by the enemy. Drink, drink. May God give you strength on your journey, and may He prevent you from falling into their hands!"

The deeper and further we went along the forest highway, the more frequently we met soldiers and dismounted riders who led their tired horses by the reins. Tired and exhausted, these soldiers trudged on ahead. Then, from the depths of the forest came a man dressed like a Soviet militiaman, leading a saddled horse by the reins, walking in our direction.

As we came face to face with him, we naturally avoided looking in his direction and continued walking at a brisk pace. But a trained soldier's eye could see he was not a "genuine" militiaman, marching west towards the enemy. He instantly gave himself away because he could not speak a word of Russian and beneath his military overcoat wore a German air force jacket with Hitler's insignia. The soldiers eyed the swastika that sat like a spider on the spy's jacket with fury.

The dispatching ceremony was brief: a bullet in the head, and Hitler's fanatic came to the end of his career. "Let it be a good start in a good season!" a Soviet soldier joked, and put his pistol back in its holster.

"Exactly the same nose and the same teeth as one of us," said a soldier, looking at the corpse. "So why are they waging such a ferocious war against us? The devil only knows!"

Finally, after long, hard effort, with blisters on our feet, (which made it many times more difficult) we crossed the old border near Volma and marched on Soviet soil. We quickly realized that the hopes we had — that the invaders would meet organized resistance at the border — were false. To our great surprise, there were no significant military units or fortifications there. We convinced ourselves that the military forces were evacuated in time and had gone deeper into the country. Here and there German planes had been shot down and resembled ominous looking burned out reptiles with yellow crosses on their long wings.

We walked through various *kolkhozes*, whose inhabitants — mainly women and old people (the young men having vanished) — offered us potatoes, bread and milk. Here and there were old wooden houses with thatched roofs. Not far from them there were big, modern houses, *kolkhoz* clubhouses, schools, and buildings with well-equipped workshops — mainly dairies with big cowsheds. We were amazed to count more than 100 cows in one of them. From a distance, the fields around the *kolkhoz*, with their fields of grain and their garden plants, looked like a huge chessboard. It was obvious the peasants in these *kolkhozes* attained a high standard of living. Their healthy red faces and neat clothing testified to it.

Those were burning hot days — the first days of July — when we arrived in the *kolkhoz* village of Nowy Dwór, about ten kilometers from Minsk. The sun scorched us mercilessly and by making us sweat, extracted the last strength from our tired bodies. We moved ahead apathetically, like shadows, and lost our ambition for further struggle. Fatalism sneaked into my soul and gained the upper hand. A feeling of melancholy pained and tormented me, squeezing my heart and constantly whispered softly to me, "Such a shame about all your sweat and toil, brother! You're stuck in a barrel."

During the course of 10 days we covered about 260 kilometers on foot, and every now and then found ourselves under fire and played "catch" with the Angel of Death. But now, 10 kilometers from Minsk, we heard the unhappy news that Minsk had been occupied by the Germans just the day before. That did not surprise us very much, since we sensed that during the past few days we had come to a dead end and it was not in our power to escape. We would have to face the enemy sooner or later.

My friend Yitzchok Epstein from Skidel was "lucky" that day. A tank crew lieutenant, who did not want to be taken prisoner by the Germans, shot himself in the local cemetery. Epstein was the first one to notice and took the pistol from the dead man, and hid it in his pocket. "It'll come in handy," he said to me gravely.

The big square next to the *kolkhoz* school was filled with soldiers from various military companies, some with weapons, others without. Many lost their units, their commanders and superiors, and were now lounging in the courtyard. There were good-natured Uzbeks, cunning Tartars, reserved Ukrainians and simple White Russians. Not all of them took this important moment seriously, and did not understand the great danger threatening their country, their families and themselves.

They sat in the bushes in little groups, scraping out the last bits of cheap rolling tobacco and breadcrumbs from their pockets, rolling it up in newspaper, and bit the thick newspaper hard with their teeth. They moistened their cigarettes with their tongues for a long time and then smoked them thoughtfully, breathed the smoke in deeply and making various plans. Some of them planned to sneak through enemy lines and get to the Berezino River. With sorrowful glances, the soldiers looked east, into the distance, where their great native land lay right under their noses — and they were cut off.

A commander and several soldiers sat crouched over a field map, quibbling over something. Suddenly the commander got up and said to the soldiers, "My friends, whoever's keen and brave enough, come with me!" Instantly a truck filled up with soldiers and set off down a side road. In less than 10 minutes, we heard heavy machine guns firing from the direction the truck had gone. Afterward it was quiet. Obviously they were ambushed not far from the village and were done for.

Other soldiers were hardly concerned. They sat, relaxed, around the campfires in the fields, cooking potatoes and beans in their steel helmets. Yet others led cows from the cowshed in the *kolkhoz*, hacked them up and roasted pieces of meat over the fire. A young cavalryman rode towards the cowshed, jumped off his horse, went into the shed and led out a young ox, quickly took his rifle and aimed at the ox's head.

"You with the gun, just wait, don't shoot!" somebody yelled in the distance. A tall captain emerged from the cornfield. His feet were covered with bugs and he carried his boots in his hands. A lieutenant was walking by his side. The captain cast a poisonous glance at the soldier and drew out a pistol from its holster. He angrily bawled out the soldier, "Why are you robbing a *kolkhoznik*? Is this, how you defend your country?"

The soldier stood like a taut string and lowered the rifle to his foot, stammering nervously: "I haven't eaten for three days, Comrade Captain. Hunger is tormenting me."

"So, because of that you have to waste a whole cow?" the captain said more quietly now and put the pistol back into its holster. "What will the *kolkhoznik* think of the Red Army — and in such a serious time too, with the enemy treading over our land? We really can't repay one of our citizens like this, because it's a crime against our own people." He looked askance at the soldier and walked away.

A wounded soldier, with a piece of shrapnel in his spine, was on the floor in the *kolkhoz* school, writhing with terrible cramps, crying like a child, groaning and begging us, "My friends, could you pass me the magnet from the field telephone that is lying there beneath the window? I want to get the shrapnel out of my back with the magnet." It was painful to look at the dying man, whom we could not really help at all. The next morning the soldier was stiff. His big glassy eyes looked fixedly up at the ceiling, as if he wanted to drill a hole in it with his last glance before dying, just to see the blue beautiful summer sky one last time.

German planes dropped yellow leaflets, that fell to the ground like autumn leaves. In saccharine and florid language, with poisonous flattery, they called on the soldiers to commit treason — to surrender and voluntarily enter captivity. They brazenly promised them freedom and a safe return to their homes. "The Soviet power has lost the war," they declared while showing the map of White Russia surrounded by a thick black line. They wanted to convince the soldiers there was no way out and that their only chance was surrender.

The boldly lettered headline read, "A permit while in captivity" and in the margin added, cunningly, that if in possession of this permit, all German military units had to recognize the bearer of the paper. It was a crafty trick, but it did not have much success. A lieutenant and approximately 10 soldiers, among them several Jews, feverishly collected discarded hand grenades, cartridges and machine pistols, several of them scattered beneath their feet. The lieutenant called out loudly to the soldiers, "Those of you who haven't given up hope and are ready to fight the occupiers, come with me. I'm an old partisan." A large group of soldiers went off with the lieutenant in the direction of the forest and quickly disappeared into its depths.

About one and a half kilometers from the *kolkhoz* school, in an open field, an unseen hand lit a green electric lamp that shone like a star in the night-time darkness. Though no one understood the meaning of the sign, it was not difficult to guess who lit the lamp. In the early morning, several soldiers with gloomy faces returned from where the lamp burned during the night. They told us they fell into the hands of the Germans the day before. But to their great surprise, the Germans did nothing to them. On the contrary, they received them cordially, offered them cigarettes, biscuits and sugar, and let them go. The soldiers were surprised about meeting the Germans and even more surprised by their kindness.

Other soldiers understood this cunning trick, spat, cursed and walked away. Still others started to interrogate the frightened soldiers, asking them to repeat their story from the beginning, exactly and with all the details. After that they conferred with each other privately in little groups.

We did not have to wait long for the results of the cunning German maneuver. A large group of tired, hungry soldiers started walking in the designated direction. "Where are you going, brother?" a soldier called out from behind a bush. For a moment they stopped to think, their heads bowed, as if they were hesitating, but that only lasted a moment. Then they quickly continued going in the same direction.

"Remember!" the same soldier called out to them, "You're walking to your death!"

No one replied. The unknown soldier was right, and his threat came true. A few months later, we heard that thousands of captured, dehydrated soldiers, suffering from typhus, were taken in garbage carts to the pits and were hurled into mass graves.

Half a day later, intense firing suddenly erupted above the little village. Bullets, from different directions whizzed above our heads. At first, we couldn't figure out where the shooting above our heads came from so suddenly. Then, in the distance, on the sand hills between the trees, we saw tanks crawling about like giant tortoises, firing in our direction. We hid in the bushes nearby and then realized that was a tactical error. The tanks were sure to crush us. So we ran to the school that was packed with many travelers, Jews and Russians, who'd run from the Germans as we did.

In the school hall it was as silent as in a cemetery. Some mothers took their little babies in their arms, as if to protect them from approaching danger. Perhaps the little child would find grace in the eyes of the unknown murderers who would be arriving at any moment. One Jew, a refugee from Poland, sat hunched in a corner on the floor, murmuring quietly to himself, as if praying, "God in Heaven, we don't have any more strength to run! For what sins are you punishing us?" He repeated his mantra continually.

It was curious that all the soldiers disappeared. I could not understand it. Not so long ago they had all been in the fields, talking comfortably among themselves, and suddenly they disappeared like demons. Then the shooting became more sporadic and soon it stopped completely.

Then the loud noise of two-stroke motorcycle engines was heard near the school. There was a burst of singing, and then it fell silent again. A familiar language that made our blood run cold was heard beneath the window. A peasant woman's husband was a lieutenant and had changed into civilian clothes not half an hour earlier, putting his pistol into the pocket of his trousers. (He sat like a little nobody next to her). She took off her white headscarf, leaned out the window and waved it around in an oddly furious manner.

Everyone was ordered to leave the school and we did. Healthy young men in mousey gray clothes, with dull, stupid faces ran back and forth, pistols in their hands, sniffing and searching for hidden weapons. They were sweaty and furious. With their cold bandit's eyes, they sized up each person and continuously shouted, "To Minsk with you! To Minsk, to the devil!"

A soldier without a cap appeared. He walked toward them with one of the yellow leaflets in his hand, babbling something. A German ran toward him, kicked him in the backside and chased him out of the way. Of course, the soldier regretted heeding the devilish, treacherous yellow flyer, but it was too late. He and several others like him, who were not particularly smart, were under guard.

We walked rapidly to Minsk. A convoy of cars carrying German military personnel drove towards us. Stiffly-dressed in their mousey gray uniforms, with their arrogant faces, the soldiers sat in their comfortable cars, with straight, erect backs, as if they had swallowed fence posts. They looked fiercely and impudently at us civilians. In their little wolves' eyes one could see their superiority complex towards "Slavs" and other people of "inferior races."

One of these "chosen people" spat in our direction and did not even turn around. Assurance and decisiveness stared out of their dull faces and it was obvious they felt very much at home on this new, freshly-conquered soil. Whether the self-confident expression on their faces was an assumed, pretended one, or whether it was a result of their narrow-mindedness and stupidity was difficult to estimate. Probably their vacant, arrogant looks stemmed from both. It was easy to read their faces. These creatures of a "higher race" brought nothing good with them.

The higher-ranking officers — Hitler's army commanders — sat in separate cars. They were stiff, as if starched, bedecked with cheap soldiers' decorations, like little bits of tinplate, crosses, twisted silver bands, silver epaulettes, caps with high crowns and lacquered peaks, with big silver shields on their chests. They were covered with swastikas on their hats, on their epaulettes, on their chests, with big swastikas on their arms. It was as if these "amulets" would protect them from danger — these mannequin officers covered with spider-like swastikas.

What was missing from these officers' uniforms and jewelry were nose rings and big earrings in each ear. Then Hitler's officers would have looked like a horde of wild African warriors. The German soldiers needed to have tin-pot, beribboned and silver-plated fetish gods, covered with swastikas from top to toe so that they could carry out every devilish order like the soldier-automatons they were, hypnotized by their bejeweled commander statues.

We caught a ride on an abandoned Red Army wagon harnessed to two horses, and we sat down and slowly continued our journey to Minsk. I met a young couple with two little children in their arms, who'd come all the way from Vilna. They looked gloomy, tired and exhausted and could hardly lift their feet. We made some room for them in the wagon. Later I found out the young man was the young popular poet, Ber Sorin who wrote sweet little poems for school children, and whose real name — as I later found out — was Beryl Levin. His wife, Sarah Yambloy, taught at a school in Vilna. These dead-tired people sat in the wagon, as if paralyzed. Their clothes were torn and dusty, their feet swollen and covered with blisters. In his jacket pocket, Ben Sorin had a little bottle of milk and every once in a while he gave it to the children to lick from.

"Daddy, give me something to eat!" the older girl, who was about six, constantly moaned. I found a piece of dry bread crust in my pocket and gave it to the hungry child. She grabbed the black, dusty piece of bread and bit into it firmly with her little white teeth. The child calmed down and tears ran from her mother's beautiful black eyes. This man is a hero, a man of iron, I thought, looking at Sorin. He undertook a dangerous and bloody journey, a considerable feat, and walked almost 200 kilometers on foot, with his children in his arms.

In my mind, his stature grew considerably. I looked at him in awe and made up my mind not to leave these people, to stay with them and to help them in their struggle. And I was a scoundrel and a coward to have run away and left my own wife and child abandoned at the edge of the abyss.

"Could I not have performed the same feat — to walk with them?" Again I saw the tear-stained face of my little daughter Bashele and heard her last plea, "Daddy, I don't want to be left alone!"

My body gave a shudder. I lowered my head, clasped Sorin's little daughter to me and kissed her on her little head. She raised her tear-swollen eyes and looked at me in a childlike way. I managed to find a piece of sugar in my pocket, kissed her wet cheeks and gave it to her. Sorin sat in the wagon, disconsolate as a bird that was shot down; silent, not saying a word, staring straight in front of him with extinguished eyes.

"We mustn't despair!" I said, trying to chase away his sadness. "Sometimes they go away as quickly as they came."

"Everything is possible," he agreed. "They'll drown in the big Russian sea. But the blow has been so heavy that we won't get rid of them that quickly," he added despairingly.

"I'm worse off," I tried to get some sympathy from him. "At least you've got your wife and children with you. I've left mine in a burning city, while I myself ran away!" He looked at me pityingly, waved his hand in a resigned way and said, "Who knows where it's best to be? We are all in hot water."

There were many recently covered graves at the side of the road, the soil freshly dug. Here and there little fence-posts were put up, and here and there were birch-wood crosses. Quickly, in haste, the gravediggers tied together two stakes with a piece of wire, forming a multiplication sign that informed the living that an unknown, foreign dead man was lying below.

One of our friends, in Yiddish, read the first name and family name of one of our compatriots off one of those grave markers. Clearly, he met his death just there, outside Minsk. Some of the graves were more lavishly adorned, covered with grass, heaps of flowers and massive crosses--their tops hung with German helmets, their graves draped in Hitler's swastika flag.

We drew some consolation from these graves in those days — they were a sign of hope for us, the hunted people, like an unknown voice whispering in our ears, "Don't despair, brothers, there is still a hand that avenges!"

I soothed my heart with these German graves and murmured to myself: "This isn't your Poland or France. You'll all stay buried here with your Brown heads." Torn documents were scattered all along the road, as well as money, guns and rifles. German soldiers drove around as if intoxicated, picking up the rifles and destroying them on the spot. Maybe their dull brains understood that the discarded rifles could quickly become dangerous weapons at their backs.

CHAPTER 5

The Minsk Ghetto

We were approaching Minsk. The city was burning. Big, powerful swirls of smoke coiled and twisted above the city, as if some devilish hand wanted to erect giant monuments, and every minute they changed shape. Here and there the devil stuck out a long, pointed red tongue and quickly hid it again in clouds of smoke. The city looked like a huge steaming cauldron. Above it there was a constant humming of airplanes like a commotion of crows. The birds of prey were whirling above the city, emitting fire and making sure the city burned to the ground.

We reached a Minsk suburb where, in an abandoned apartment in a wooden house, we found temporary shelter. It was once the apartment of a railway man, who evacuated in time. There was a bed, a table, a sofa, the most needed dishes and a sack of dried biscuits on the wall, which we consumed on the spot. We lay down on the floor, tired, half-dead, and tried to rest.

I soon sold both horses and the wagon to Kolinik, a Christian night watchman, who gave me a loaf of black bread for them. He promised that as soon as he earned something, he would not forget us.

"So, how do you get on with your new masters?" I asked him cautiously. "Not bad for the time being," he answered simply. "So far, so good."

"So how do they treat the civilian population?" I asked further. "It depends who," he started to say, but then broke off and didn't finish his sentence when he realized that there were Jews in our group.

"But there's no need to worry," he tried to comfort us. "They seem to be quite intelligent and good people. They walk around nicely dressed, make way in the middle of the road, wash to the waist and clean their fingernails. I've got the impression that we'll be able to live with them," he concluded optimistically.

We felt strangely disconcerted after this conversation with Kolinik. His careless tone of voice and happy face were like handfuls of salt in our wounds, even though we did not feel any hostility towards us from this simple White Russian. And yet, his self-confident mood, his quiet thoughts about his own fate and his simple indifference to our precarious future, moved us to the depths of our souls.

We could not believe that this simple watchman had made peace with the deadly enemy of his people; that he believed in the humanity of the "Brown Shirts" and hoped to live with them. At any rate, we got no satisfaction from our conversation with Kolinik, and after that felt our misery even more keenly. Silently, as if we had been whipped, we remained sitting on the floor.

I decided to go and find my wife's brother Notki Gordon, who had been living in Minsk for about 20 years. He had visited me a year before the war. I hesitated going to see him and wondered if I should show my face at all. He would surely not understand me and would not forgive me for abandoning his sister and running off to save myself. He would not want to believe anything I said and would chase me away. And he would be right.

Anyway, whatever would happen, I had to see him. I made up my mind. I would try to explain to him. Maybe he would understand me and empathize with my suffering. Maybe he would even forgive me and give me some good advice. Like a thief, I made my way down the bustling New Moscow Street.

My typically Semitic face immediately revealed I was Jewish. With my head down, I walked quickly, casting brief, furtive glances to either side and ahead of me. German military personnel were in the streets like dark swarms of locusts; they were stretched out in all the nooks and crannies — they were pedestrians and cyclists. With their rifles leaning on saw-horses, they sat at the street-corners, smoking, laughing and getting sunburned. Others stood at the water pumps, half-naked, and washed themselves, shaving and cleaning their nails with various instruments made of nickel.

Burned-out houses with black, smoldering walls and cement balconies with iron railings, hung precariously above people's heads along the streets. Cracked glass, torn and trodden books, pieces of geographical maps, dented globes, an upended Royal typewriter and loads of school benches and cupboards were tossed to the curb. It probably all came from the undamaged elementary school nearby. Looking out of its windows were the stupid faces of German soldiers, who had converted the school into military barracks.

No, I decided again, these people don't possess any spark of culture or civilization. They tread on the world with their hobnail boots, without a sense of culture or aesthetics. They polish their nails and shave their chins, just like any other bodily need. They probably stole their little manicure sets and bottles of cologne in France, and the purpose of their grooming is at best "a show of pride in their superman German master-race culture."

On one street-corner an announcement was been posted, the size of a notebook page, in White Russian. In bold letters it proclaimed the "happy news" that just after the arrival of the Germans in Minsk, 100 Jews were arrested as speculators, communists who viewed White Russian population with contempt and that they had been executed. Further down on the paper, they added, like salt for flavor, that the day had finally come when German arms liberated the White Russian people from collective Jewish rule.

White Russian civilians walked past, sniffed at the text, spat and went away. I did not finish reading this piece of toilet paper. I felt scalded, as if I had been one of those 100 Jews. The devil is starting his tricks, I thought, and he does it quickly and cunningly. He tries to harp on a delicate and dangerous thread, awakening a desire for pogroms in White Russian hearts and infusing the embittered civilian population with a lust for innocent Jewish blood. Would he succeed? I asked myself in anguish. But I could not read anything in the frozen and reserved faces of the White Russians furtively wandering through the streets.

I soon found my brother-in-law's apartment. His wife, broken-hearted and tear-swollen, told me he had been in a camp for a week. As soon as the Germans occupied Minsk, they gathered all the male inhabitants between 18 and 45 years of age and kept them surrounded by police officers in an open field under the sun, not allowing them any food or water. They mocked them and made them suffer tormenting thirst. They killed many of them with clubs; others were shot, and they enacted various devilish orgies on the victims.

They kept the White Russians in this hell for nine days and the Jews for 18. Then they let them go. Young people could hardly crawl. Dehydrated, burned by the sun and with their hair wildly unkempt, these living dead were led home on the arms of their sisters and parents.

With tears in her eyes, my sister-in-law listened to the sorrows of my heart, comforted me and cautiously reproached me for running away on my own. She gave me some food and told me about the gruesome agony they lived through during the past few days. I turned around, wanting to look at my face in the mirror above the sofa, but started to tremble.

Above the mirror there was a picture of my daughter Bashele. I grabbed the picture frantically, brought it close to my eyes that were running with tears. My throat became tight, as if someone was strangling me. I moved the picture even closer, and looked at the dear face of my daughter, but she was all hazy, because my eyes were immediately clouded with tears.

"My child, my dear Bashele," I wailed with anguish. "Who knows, if you're still a…" I did not complete my lament and continued, "Your Daddy has betrayed you, promised you to bring you nice things and ran away from you like a coward. My dear child!"

I clasped the photograph to my heart, shaking with torment. "I swear a sacred oath that I will come back to you and beg you for forgiveness!"

I said good-bye to my sister-in-law, hid the photograph in my inside coat pocket and went back to my friends. An elemental power was now in my coat pocket, stinging me, burning me and sobbing childishly, "Come home, Daddy, you've promised me! Come now. I'm waiting for you!"

Soon hunger bared its claws. The loaf of bread I received for the horses went quickly and Kolinik did not want to give us more. The next day, he arrived, gloomy and angry. He told us he was disappointed in the Germans: They had taken a horse from him in the morning and repaid him with a fist to the head. "There are all sorts of sheep in a flock, not just rotten ones. And in fact, they've left me one horse after all," he comforted himself.

"If only you were right," I suggested to him naively. "I'm afraid that none of the Germans will be all that impressive." I cautiously explained to him what I meant, gesturing with my hands. He did not answer me at all, but went away lost in thought. He was probably thinking whether only half of the flock was rotten or whether they were all lousy. In any case, two days later he came back. This time he had been hit hard in the eye and his lower lip was swollen and hanging crookedly. With his eyes to the ground, he told us that two

Germans approached him and babbled something in their devilish language, probably telling him to unhitch the horse from the wagon.

He did not understand quickly enough with what they wanted from him. So they honored him with a punch in the eye and knocked him in the teeth. Then he understood they wanted the horse, and he gave it to them. He remained silent for a while, then suddenly spat and added that they were all parasites and rat scabs. This time Kolinik's words offered us some comfort. They showed us that the facts convinced him and he was now politically conscious.

Our hunger nagged us to find a crust of bread, whether from acquaintances or strangers. In those days Minsk overflowed with refugees. Workers or intellectuals, it made no difference — they all went from house to house, looking for something to eat, at least a spoonful of some cooked food. The population of Minsk was not miserly and shared its last bite with the hungry. It was only in those tragic days that I had the opportunity to perceive the good-hearted souls of Gorki's people.

On a scorching hot day in July, a friend and I stumbled into a small wooden house, hungry and lethargic. An old woman sat at a table eating something and understood from the look on our faces that hunger tormented us. She got up from her chair, gave us a wooden spoon, pushed her bowl of borsht at us and insisted that we eat. We wanted to withdraw, claiming that we just wanted to ask for a drink of water. But the old woman did not back away and insisted that we sit down at the table.

"But little mother, you won't have anything to eat yourself tomorrow," I said stubbornly. "Eat, little doves," she pleaded with us. "Who knows, if my Alyosha is still alive…" And she pressed the wooden spoon into my hand. I held the simple Russian wooden spoon as if it was sacred, put several spoonfuls of borsht into my mouth and looked at the old woman, searching in her features for any similarities to my own mother. She found an egg in her henhouse, pressed it into my hand, and when we left, told us: "When you're hungry again, don't be ashamed, for God's sake, come back."

We were deeply moved by our experience in that small house with the unknown Russian mother.

Severe blows began raining down on the unfortunate Jews of Minsk. Every day new orders were hung on the fences like carcasses, one demand more poisonous and lethal than the next. Then came orders regarding the sign of shame — the Yellow Star. There were orders to relocate to the ghetto, orders regarding various contributions and many other things.

It was painful to wear the small, round piece of yellow material, eight centimeters in diameter, in accordance with the order. It was a heavy moral burden on one's shoulders that felt like it weighed 10 stones. The first time I put this sign of shame on to go out into the street, I felt something I could not have imagined in my life. The mark burned my back and chest, as if I had been pierced through and through with knitting needles, and I was screaming out loud from my bent back.

"Attention, here comes a Jew! Watch out for him! Don't speak to him! Avoid him! Don't smile at him! Don't touch him! But you may hit him, beat him black and blue, slap him, kick him and spit in his face. He is an outlaw; he is the lowest form of life. You can ridicule and humiliate him because he wears the yellow star and no one will stick up for him."

Those were the thoughts in my head whenever I wore the star. Like a criminal, I ran quickly through back streets, cut through various courtyards and twisting alleyways. I hurried to the *Judenrat* on New Moscow Street, opposite Respublica Street. A young Russian walking on the opposite pavement in the other direction noticed my furtive "thief-like" walk and shouted out to me: "Why are you running, my little friend? Your star will soon be torn off!" I raised my head for a second and saw a smiling face. For a moment, the heavy load on my back became lighter.

I straightened my back, replied with a smile to this unknown man, who had felt my deep anguish and had offered me a word of comfort in such a singular and disguised manner. I looked at the yellow star again and understood that I was still a human being after all.

Many Jews, young and old, stood in front of the *Judenrat*, housed in a low, half-ruined little building. With sad and gloomy faces, they listened to the mournful speech of the *Judenrat* leader, the engineer Mushkin. He spoke in Russian, under the open sky, and informed his listeners about the tragic situation facing the Jews of Minsk. He aroused compassion and implored people not to let newly orphaned children die of hunger; to share their last piece of bread with them or at least to give them a cup of cereal.

"My Jewish brothers!" he shouted with a mournful voice. "Remember that our situation is extremely serious. We don't know what tomorrow may bring — not a lot of good in any case. Be united, all of you, look after the innocent, hungry orphans. They are the children of each and every one of us, because their parents died first and foremost for being Jews!"

He wiped his eyes with his handkerchief, broke off his speech of "Lamentations" for a moment and then continued: "We have received an order to pay a horrendously high tax, far beyond our capability, and I don't know what to do. It is five kilograms of gold and 15 kilograms of silver. I don't know whether one can find five Jews who even have that amount of bread these days.

"This demand smells of blood. If we don't get it for them, I don't know how many victims it will cost us. They won't let us off. It'll be a pretext for killing hundreds and maybe even thousands of victims! You must understand, brothers, what kind of situation we are in. I don't see any consolation in our hopeless situation."

He stopped talking, mingled with the crowd and then went back into the *Judenrat*. For a while the masses stood there as if frozen, with dead faces and extinguished eyes. High up on the hill above the *Judenrat* stood a prison with a high brick wall. Quick, short bursts of machine-gun fire, like the stutter of a sewing machine, continuously came from the other side and made the half-insensible crowds realize that Mushkin's speech was well-founded, that it really did smell of blood.

Feverishly the Minsk Jews moved to the ghetto. The deadline was close. By August 1, 1941, all the Jews had to move to the exactly demarcated narrow streets at one end of the city, near the Jewish cemetery and Jubilee Square.

Bent double, young and old carried their poor possessions on their backs, in sacks and bundles, to the designated place. The most important and necessary things for the household were loaded onto broken prams — pots, glasses, plates, a coat rack. An old-fashioned clock beat time like a metronome as it was carried in a pram. There were used and worn-out combs and cleaning brushes that in normal times would have been relegated to the rubbish heap, and a few other things for the immediate needs of the household.

This tragic procession towards the narrow streets of the ghetto by the proud Jews of Minsk — who for 20 years had not experienced the bitter yoke of persecuted Jews — became deeply engraved in my mind. They walked like mourners at a funeral, their heads bowed, the brand of shame on their backs, mocking them. With measured steps, as if saying good-bye to the broad streets of Minsk for the last time, they bore their remaining few poor possessions with their heavy heads.

I could not understand why they had not evacuated further into the country. After all, they had seven days' notice. Why did large numbers of them remain in Minsk? Did they not reckon with the cruelty of the enemy? Did they overestimate the actual military strength of their native country? Did they not want to break up their little nests and wander down unknown roads in their vast homeland during these difficult days of the war? I was never able to get any definitive answer to these questions.

Judging their situation dispassionately, I understood one had to be an exceptional person, to be daring and ambitious and have a powerful will to live to foresee everything and be willing to leave behind the labor of decades, to brush everything aside with one sweep of the hand. It could well be that specifically Jewish fatalism was decisive — clinging blindly to faith and hoping, that this time, too, one could probably survive. (To their great misfortune, fate betrayed them and hope deceived them, just like it did all Jews).

During the move to the ghetto, I happened into an unknown house in a street that was now "free of Jews," to find something to eat.

The new owner of the house, a Christian, and the former owner, a Jew, sat at the table. The Jewish man finished writing something on a piece of paper and pushed it towards the Christian to sign. At the same time, the Jewish man read the paper out loud again. The paper was a contract, describing precisely which objects and furniture in the household the Jewish man was leaving to his Christian friend, on condition that after the liberation, when the Jew came back from the ghetto, his friend would return all these above-mentioned items to him, whole and undamaged. The Jew put the paper into his inside coat pocket, said a cordial good-bye to his friend and went out.

It was a golden time for thieves, murderers and other criminals the Germans freed from prison. They now had another category of people who would torment, mock and steal from the innocent inhabitants of the ghetto. The allies of these criminals were the ethnic Germans, who during a famine sometime ago at the river Volga, where their autonomous region was, had immigrated all the way to Minsk. They all had guns and black forage caps on their heads, and those freshly-baked policemen and their faithful assistant hangmen poured out their stupid and senseless wrath in a newly pumped-up anti-Jewish pogrom in the ghetto.

Every night they attacked different houses in the ghetto, beating the Jews black and blue with murderous blows and stealing everything they could find. Every night, fits of crying and sobbing would disturb the night-time gloom. After several gunshots, everything would sink back into silence and the darkness of the night, as if nothing had happened. Mainly they robbed people at night. During the day they would not dare to, not because they were ashamed or were afraid of the German authorities — by no means — but simply because during daytime, in the bright sunshine, only the superior race alone, the Germans, had the right to rob and steal, and no one was allowed to disturb them.

Very confidently, coldly and methodically, the Germans looked through and felt everything and took whatever was valuable to them. Those things became gifts like "war trophies" for their lovers and friends in Germany. After the daytime raids, the policemen came at night like hyenas and robbed the Jews of whatever remained. A bit later, they started catching people in the streets of the ghetto. As if they had sprung up from underground, the Brown Shirted bandits would suddenly appear, seize big and small groups, regardless of age or gender, and mercilessly beat them black and blue. They would drag sick people out of their beds and vanish with their human booty. The little streets of the ghetto were filled with wailing and lamentations after such "actions." It seemed as if even the cobblestones cried over the fate of those who had just disappeared.

There was no point in walking around, because one needed to have a work permit. Without one, a person could easily fall victim to an "action," and my hunger finally forced me to get one. I went to work at the former tailoring factory, "October," the clothing warehouse for the Air Fleet, Second Commando. It had not been easy for me to make this decision, which meant having a hand in the process of self-destruction. But hunger tormented me, and the immediate dangerous situation drove me, like hundreds of other Jews, to go and work for the enemy.

Deep in my heart I decided my "contribution" to the Brown Shirts would be minimal and possibly — if the opportunity arose — damaging and antagonistic. As a carpenter, it was quite easy for me to sneak in to work. The supervision was lax and no one disturbed me, even if I did not lift a finger for whole days, but simply paced up and down in the courtyard with a saw in my hand, in order to get the attention of the inspectors and show them I was "very busy." I also had the opportunity to prick up my ears to hear what the airborne regiment soldiers who came to get their uniforms were saying.

With deep satisfaction, I overheard a conversation between two drivers who just arrived from Smolensk. One told the other about the huge battles going on there. "Our pilots don't have a minute's rest," he told his friend. "They don't even have time to get a drink of water. The Reds are devils and their artillery spits fire like a volcano," he concluded with a gloomy expression – to my great joy.

"Wait! Wait!" I thought, as I pretended to check the teeth of my saw, and looked at them furtively. "You wait! You'll all be burned in this fire! You won't be wanting any more *Lebensraum*."

I needed to adopt a cautious approach to keep myself from talking politics with the soldiers, especially with senior officers, who were civil servants and businessmen by profession, as well as small landowners. Typical soldiers were mostly workers and simple people — narrow-minded, deluded, incited nationalists, puffed-up patriots of their native land, fanatic militarists and blind believers in the power of their *Führer* — in whose hands murder weapons were certainly lethal. Drunk from victories in Western and Southern Europe, they were convinced of their *Führer's* genius. They believed that in Eastern Europe no one but their *Führer* would be victorious. Many of them firmly believed this and even calculated arithmetically that in exactly two weeks' time Moscow would fall.

Their calculation was very simple: It was about 800 kilometers to Moscow. The German tanks covered about 50 kilometers a day. So it was very clear that it would take about two weeks, and the war would be over. From day to day they constantly delayed the day of the victory and hoped to go home after that. These soldiers were no great politicians. They put all the blame for the war on England, on the capitalists and on the Jews, who had taken over the whole world, who had foisted the Treaty of Versailles on them and had taken their right to live away from them.

"And why am I guilty?" I would often ask one of them as if I was naive. He would choke on his answer like an idiot, but finally would blurt out that, in fact, I was not really guilty myself, but because I had a rich uncle in America or in England, I was guilty all the same. As in Ivan Krylov's[4] fable, "The Wolf and the Sheep" — where the shepherd hires the wolf and the sheep begin to

---

4 Ivan Andreyevich Krylov (1769-1844) Russian writer of fables.

disappear — this was more or less how the thought processes of the average German military man operated.

After such conversations, I often felt the urge to tell the German soldiers off and reveal the whole truth — that Jewish blood was the cheapest commodity in the world, that the axles of the huge war machine were greased with Jewish blood, that our blood was given to the soldiers to drink, even before they went to the front — in order to arouse the beast inside them — and that for generations, various devils and dark leaders had been bathing in our blood.

For thousands of years we had been a wandering nation, scattered like dust under people's feet, dust upon which the heavy wheels of history turned throughout different tragic eras. This and only this would have been the real truth about our "guilt" in the present war.

A German soldier called me into his room. The floor boards were broken, and he asked me to repair them. The national emblem of Hitler's empire, a bird of prey with vast, outstretched wings, big claws and a healthy beak, stood above a globe, on which the swastika was painted in black, with a bold inscription, "Everything for Germany" painted on the wall above his bed. The picture looked down from the wall like a malevolent icon. Apparently during sleepless nights this dull soldier's head drew spiritual sustenance from such an idol.

My assistant was Chaim Alexandrovich, a compatriot of mine who managed to get to Minsk. He was an old revolutionary and well-known figure in the former Poland and western regions of White Russia. When I met him in Minsk he was bloated from hunger, and I appointed him my assistant at work, where he received bread and soup. He would not get into any conversations with the soldiers and advised me not to talk to them. He would look at them fiercely and often tell me that it was unnecessary to waste words on them. "There's only one kind of argument for them and that's a bullet," he would say.

There was a big new pistol on the bedroom table. I did not pay much heed to the gun and repaired the floor calmly. Chaim went in and out of the room a couple of times, helping me with my work, and eventually the floor was finished. I returned the key to the German and went back to the workshop. Early next morning, the German called me into his room and told me his pistol had disappeared. Maybe I knew something about it?

I was surprised by his question.

He instantly noticed my surprise, changed his tone and tried a different way of working on me. "You'll get 10 loaves of bread," he said to me, "if you find my pistol for me." I soon found a plausible explanation and suggested that it was probably one of his comrades, who was in the room while we worked there, who took his pistol away.

"I don't need your pistol myself. I'm a ghetto Jew and I thank God, if nobody bothers me," I tried to make him understand. "And you didn't hide it under the floor boards?" he asked me gravely. I took my axe and offered to rip the floor open to show him that that was not the case.

He let me go that time, roaring like an animal, "I will have bad luck." (Only much later, when I was in the forests, did I receive news that Alexandrovich was the commander of a partisan unit and had nearly 200 German scalps to his "credit," as well as about 10 troop trains. The beginning of his "forest career" had been that stolen pistol).

It was difficult to work on an empty stomach. The piece of bread and the little drop of watery lunchtime soup mixed with sweepings of leaves and some other "unspecified" ingredients, could hardly give me enough strength to work.

The cook, a former criminal, first distributed the thicker portions from the pot among his Russian worker acquaintances. Then he served the women, the Russian ones first, of course, and the last thin watery soup he gave to the Jews. Apart from this, he stole the miserable little piece of meat that should have fed almost 300 people. So it was no surprise that one had to be cunning and find other ways to sustain one's sinful flesh.

Before work in the morning, all the workers lined up in groups according to their trades, and a German would give each one a little token to get his portion of bread, tobacco and soup. But I would craftily sneak into a second, third and fourth group, to get additional food tokens. That way, I had enough bread for myself and to help my hungry friends, though I was risking my neck for it. But it was worth it. Afterwards the head cook would rack his brains and wonder where the food went.

"There are no more than 300 workers, but 305 are guzzling the food," he would grumble angrily. He deduced that someone was probably copying the tokens. So he started to distribute stamped tin numbers. But in one of the attics, I found a number of these little tin badges and so again I was well-supplied with bread for quite some time.

And often — may I be forgiven for this — I would end up "attacking" the peasant's horse and tearing a little chunk of bread the German would feed it, out from under its teeth. At the same time I would stroke the horse and make it understand that it would be able to digest potato peels just as well. Once, when we finished working, the gates were locked and the German administration searched the workers thoroughly, to see if anybody was carrying anything away from the factory. Instantly, spools of thread, scraps of material and other tailor's equipment were scattered on the floor. None of the Jewish workers was caught, God forbid. They had "gotten clean" in time.

We heard the head inspector's voice. He was screaming wildly, dragging the cook, who was carrying a big pot of meat in his hand, by his collar. "Look, who's guzzling your meat!" the head inspector screamed. He honored the cook with a fist in the head several times and loudly informed us: "We'll shoot him very soon."

The interpreter, a non-commissioned officer, quickly translated the "good news" into Russian. The cook made such a wild grimace that one had to be harder than iron not to laugh. But the incident ended quite differently. They merely gave him a good beating on the mouth, which did not bother us in the slightest. On the contrary, it delighted us that this freshly-baked Aryan cook got paid back by his Aryan masters for the Aryan lunches that he served us. Finally, as a bonus, he got a boot up his backside and howling, ran from the courtyard.

From day to day, the situation in Minsk grew more critical. Hour by hour, the leash around the necks of the Jews of Minsk was drawn tighter. Constantly, every day, more of my acquaintances disappeared in the "actions." Very clearly, the Minsk Jews saw before them the abyss that was going to swallow up everyone sooner or later. But the great force of hope still kept the unfortunates alive.

In the ghetto different rumors and versions of events — true and imaginary — were passed from person to person. Somewhere a troop landing had taken place; a large part of the enemy army was surrounded; "they" were retreating in panic all along the line, and the like. All these rumors were an expression of what the persecuted Jews wished to see. But time and events went on at their own slow pace and deflated those premature hopes. People's eyes had become sharp and they closely observed the constant mass movement of the German armies through the streets of the city.

One evening someone stormed forcefully into the house, shouting: "Come and see! They're retreating!!! They're fleeing from the front in their battered trucks!!!" Our joy and surprise were indescribable. We quickly went out to Nyemiga Street, and indeed a certain number of bullet-riddled trucks crawled along, away from the front, and that gave some hothead a reason to insist that the enemy was departing. Utterly deceived, heads bent, we went back to the ghetto with a deeper depression in our hearts than before.

My friend Alexandrovich laughed at us sarcastically and said: "Don't believe in quick salvation. The war is long and hard, and if you want to live, you will have to do something about it."

The streets of Minsk were alive with the volume of military traffic. Long convoys of military vehicles and trucks, all kinds of artillery, tanks and petrol tankers were constantly and unendingly winding their way through the streets like poisonous snakes, through Sovetska Street, following the highway to Smolensk. It was frightening to look at these creatures, who carried the destruction of human civilization in their armory; to look at those haughty manners, leaden faces, low foreheads and expressionless eyes. Decorated and beribboned with the profanity of swastikas, they made everyone shudder when they thought of what this "higher race" was capable of doing to the world.

During the night, one could often hear shooting from the busy streets, and the next day there would be an announcement by the city commander that a military transport had been fired at from such and such a house, and 20 people from that aforementioned house were going to be held responsible. Such announcements were common. The Germans also appointed guards to keep watch over the field telephone line at night. One person had to keep watch over a hundred meters' length of the telephone line — he had to run up and down the hundred meters continuously, while holding the wire in his hand, so that no one could tear it apart during the night. If they succeeded, the guard would have had to pay with his head.

CHAPTER 6

Finding a Way Back to Grodno

The environment began to smell of resistance and the partisans started to show signs of life. Once, when I finished my day's work, a German driver told me to repair his car. I applied myself to this task and in the course of a few hours finished it, and was given a small loaf of bread and some tobacco. As usual, I went home to the ghetto through the back streets. When I arrived in the courtyard in front of my apartment, I heard that a gang of Gestapo agents came and took almost everyone from our house away with them — the majority of them young people. Despite their work permits, they were beaten black and blue, kicked and led away to an unknown destination.

In the street all hell broke loose. In every house people cried, grieved, wrung their hands in sorrow, beat their heads against the wall and wailed over the living dead. Nothing else tormented me as much as the cries of the little children, who filled every corner of the house with squealing and weeping. There was no place to hide from it and it broke my heart, lancing my spirit. Those little children, who had not yet seen the world properly, had not yet experienced 10 spring times and were already swallowing bitter tears, wailing over their fate and their fathers, who had been carried off.

I stretched out on my bed, and buried my head deep in my pillow, so as not to hear the weeping. But it was in vain. Their wailing tore pieces of living flesh from me. I understood that foolish words of comfort calmed older people. But children who suddenly lost their fathers could not be consoled by clever words. In the weeping of these children I heard the voice of my own little child, who wept just like that when I ran away, and was surely still weeping.

Involuntarily, I put my hand in my inside coat pocket, touched the glossy paper and took out Bashele's picture. How imploringly she looked at me! It seemed to me I saw teardrops on her childish little cheeks and that I heard her weeping, "Daddy, come home now!"

I rolled some thick cigar tobacco into a piece of newspaper, and breathed the bitter smoke deeply into the whole of my lungs. Then I began to make plans to go home. There is a strange power in tobacco smoke. It makes one's thoughts clearer and brings distant goals nearer. It helps one to think logically and temporarily creates the illusion of solving insoluble problems.

The way back to Grodno was blocked as if with seven locks. There was mortal danger at every turn. The yellow star and ghetto were poisoning our blood, crushing the individual self, chaining will power and mocking human sensibility. But despite all this, in my mind I plucked off the yellow star, straightened the back of the ghetto Jew and decided to pull myself firmly together, to cross the farthest depths and go back home. I approached this matter very cautiously, making all kinds of calculations and plans and looked for the most direct course to take. There was no question of going back on foot. A group of Jews who left on foot were stopped by Poles who murdered them in Rakov, at the Polish-Soviet border,

Disguising myself as a Christian was equally impossible. My appearance and language would betray me. Going by train was impossible. But then I had an idea. I would try to "sniff out" where in the west the trucks loaded with military clothing and trophies were headed when they left our factory. The thoughts flew through my head. In my imagination I saw myself hidden in such a truckload of goods. But I did not want to think too much about it, for I didn't want to draw the Evil Eye to this "cunning idea." And with such sweet thoughts I fell asleep with the newspaper cigar in my mouth, as if I had been struck dead.

I do not know if I slept for long, but I felt someone rolling me from side to side and could barely make out the voice of my landlady. I opened my eyes. She stood bent over me, frightened to death, shaking as if in convulsions, and attempted to revive me in a broken voice, "Faster! Faster! Get up, Reizer. 'They' are in the next courtyard! Do you hear them beating people?"

The sun, like me, had only just risen and its rays came through the low windows of the little half-ruined wooden houses in the ghetto, houses that were squeezed together, one against the other. Wrapped in rags, people snored in their narrow grave-like apartments, dreaming of free, careless days. Scattered at our feet or hanging on the wall was the clown's clothing with the yellow star, that we had to wear to taste the bitter yoke of the tormented Jew. Torn and broken shoes stood beneath our beds and warned: "Soon it will get cold and we won't be able to help you at all!"

A child who lost his father the previous day, turned and tossed restlessly, holding his little hands in a strange position, as he had two days earlier, when he slept in his father's arms. The sun was not miserly, casting sheaves of rays to brighten that which was called "living" in the ghetto.

I dressed as quickly as a devil. We could hear the blows from the other courtyard. It sounded like the clapping of planed-down boards. Restless hobnail boots grated on the cobblestone pavement, coming closer to our house. I ran outside as if I had been shot, hardly managing to put on my padded coat, and held my work permit ready in my hand. With bold steps, I went out of the gate. Opposite me stood a devil in a military uniform and helmet, with a machine gun in his hands. He heard my footsteps and turned around like a mannequin.

"Come here!" he roared.

I went toward him briskly and looked straight into his bandit's face. The brute roared: "Where are you going?"

"To the air force clothing depot."

"Your papers!" he roared.

I hurriedly showed him my papers. He looked at them, thought for a moment and let me go. I took the route through the Jewish cemetery. More devils with machine guns stood hidden between the graves. Some of them asked for my papers again and wondered why the previous guard let me through. Others were probably surprised at my upright, bold and non-Jewish way of walking and left me in peace.

Only Russian workers went to the factories. I quickly went to see the boss and informed him that the ghetto was surrounded by the Gestapo, that all workers were being held and that they would soon be taken away. He got into his car quickly and headed in the direction of the ghetto. A few hours later, the workers came back, frightened, battered, some without their hats. They thanked me with all their heart for letting the boss know what was happening, leading to their liberation.

I could feel the ground beneath our feet getting hot, and even if I managed to escape that time, I would surely fail the next. I could not waste any time, but had to carry out my plan.

What should I do for my plan to be a success? I wondered. There was only one goal for me — and it ranked higher than all my other wishes: to go home to Frumke and Bashele. My longing for them did not let me rest. I smoked one cigarette after another, breathing in the smoke, carried along on the trusty wings of my dream.

"What are you thinking?" asked my friend Alexandrovich. I poured my bitter heart out and told him about yearning to go home to my wife and child. He looked at me indifferently and had no advice to give me.

Two Germans in black uniforms entered the workshop. At first I thought they were Gestapo, but they told us they were Dutch drivers traveling the Minsk-Warsaw route, carrying clothing and other cargo. At those words I shuddered and asked them the same question again. To my greatest joy, I got the same answer. They asked me to do some work for them, but my head was reeling with thoughts, and though I began to do their work, I was so confused I grabbed the saw instead of the hammer and the chisel instead of the pliers.

I tried to loosen their tongues, and asked them if they passed through Grodno and what the city looked like. They happily answered me, described how the town looked, and I was convinced they told the truth. While they spoke, they added that in a few days' time they would be going back to Warsaw via Grodno.

That was the right moment. I put aside my tools and told them a tale out of the Arabian Nights. I said that I was not from Minsk, that I had been in the sanatorium to get some rest when the war seized me at the station on my way home — that is to Grodno, where I had a wife and a child. I was torn away from them and going crazy with longing. I showed them Bashele's picture and said, "I know that you've got wives and children in Holland, who long for you and want to see you again. I think you understand me. At the moment we are friends and have only one desire! That's why I'm asking you to do me this really vital favor, not to turn me down, but to take me in your truck along this 'little stretch of road' to Grodno."

I put the whole force of my fierce desire to go home into my words. I stressed every syllable, and looked straight into their eyes, as if I wanted to hypnotize them into saying "Yes." It was possible that those simple Dutchmen could not bear the moral force of my argument or maybe they felt my passion, and they agreed to take me along.

My joy was indescribable. I would rediscover my lost happiness, though I had no guarantees that my wife and child were safe. The constant reports I'd heard from the region were not happy at all. At that time, one believed everything and took news at face value, but I had superhuman faith and hoped that Frumke and Bashele were alive and waiting for me. After being torn from them for a hundred days in stormy times, I was going to experience great happiness at our reunion.

CHAPTER 7

Shtetlach on the Way

It was September 20, 1941. The "*Hapel-Blitz*" flew swiftly from Minsk to Warsaw. The truck route passed through Vilna on its way to Grodno and through a few smaller towns that once were vibrant Jewish communities. I sat between bundles of soldiers' old uniforms that were bloody and full of holes, and looked at God's world with gloom.

The golden autumn stretched over the vast, newly-harvested White Russian fields, gardens and orchards. Evergreen masses of conifers stood in their century-old positions, as if they hid secrets in their depths. The sun looked mildly from the clear blue sky and with its kind autumn rays caressed my worn-out face and stirred up hope. The pleasantly fragrant autumn air revived me and secretly consoled me. All was not yet lost.

The sides of the road were littered with destroyed German tanks and overturned trucks, proof of earlier battles, heavily fought. Through the windows, I could see crosses of birchwood hung with military helmets, and half-rotten rags with swastikas were fluttering above them flying by. They reminded the world that nighttime bandits had gotten their just desserts.

Strangely, I felt I had to count exactly how many of those graves there were from Minsk to Vilna. I tried to count them, but every once in a while I lost count and started all over again. The beautiful landscape did not let me forget I was a Jew. Near Jewish *shtetlach*, Jews with Stars of David on their clothes were at work on the highway. They were gloomy, skinny, black from the dust, breaking stones and carrying stretchers full of sand. Their glances were dark.

They noticed the truck with curiosity and cast suspicious glances at me. I tried waving at them, but they gazed at me foolishly and talked among themselves, probably trying figure out why a civilian was waving to them from a German truck.

Soon the sun slowly bowed out in the west and disappeared below the purple-pink horizon. It quickly became dark. My body trembled from the chill autumn wind. I put on my Russian padded coat, my only possession, smoked some home-cured root tobacco, and once again was worlds away, flying on the trusty wings of my dream and traveling back to my lost happiness.

The further I traveled, the stronger my curiosity became. My longing to see Frumke and Bashele as soon as possible welled up in me, though various gloomy thoughts about their fate tormented me. Deep in my heart a spark of hope glowed, that I would still find them alive; that they were waiting for me; that I would kiss them and ask them for forgiveness.

As we got closer to Grodno, little flames emerged from the distant darkness, and then we came to a halt near Oszmiana. The drivers stopped their truck, talked quietly among themselves and told me they were taking the truck to a military site for the night. They told me not to move around in the courtyard and draw attention to myself. I thanked them cordially, crawled deep inside the truck among the clothes and hid myself well.

Somewhere planes buzzed in the sky and shots could be heard in the distance. The vast sky was blue and cold, but my hiding place felt safe, and in its warmth I quickly fell asleep. When I woke with the dawn, the drivers were standing outside the truck, busying themselves with the engine. The night had been cold and it was not easy to start the engine. A tractor was coupled to the truck and it dragged us onto the highway. Then the truck continued under its own steam.

Near Mołodeczno masses of military men appeared on the highway. They were German infantry who carried their weapons in blue-painted wagons pulled by horses. High-caliber cannons, long-necked anti-aircraft guns and machine guns were all piled into them chaotically. Other wagons carried warped chairs, benches, cupboards and other furniture. The elite officers sat in separate wagons, smoking and talking comfortably among themselves, exactly as if going to a village wedding or on an outing.

From their physical appearance and manner, it was obvious they were not German. They were more similar to Semites. All of them were dark and sunburned, had curly hair and Semitic noses, and gesticulated with their hands — just like Jews. There was no trace of the pure Germanic race. The only thing German about them was their uniforms. I was curious to know who those fighters were, walking so casually toward gruesome slaughter.

Our truck stopped and cautiously I asked my drivers if the men were Italians. "You think so?" one of them asked mockingly, pointing at the marching soldiers. "They are Spaniards." He also added with contempt: "They are not fighters–they are guzzlers!"

Involuntary I smiled, and thought of Cervantes. "Cervantes! Where are you? You'd be really proud of the new Don Quixotes in the Second World War."

It turned out that they were Franco's Blue Battalion and perished in the battle for Leningrad.

We approached Vilna. Church spires, factory chimneys and tops of towers slowly emerged on the horizon. Respectable little houses moved toward us, bathed in a yellowish autumn green. Long rows of chestnut and maple trees, with yellowish crowns half-shed, stood at the side of the highway. People were coming and going at a brisk pace. I stared at the people, their clothes and faces. Were they Jews? What would they tell me? Were they exposed to the same tortures as the Jews of Minsk? My heart wanted to talk and tell my brothers in Vilna how the Jews of Minsk were living.

I visited Vilna once. Vilna Jews had a reputation for being filled with good-hearted, generous people, fine souls and simple, guileless folk. The Chaimkes, Shmerkes and Rochelehs of Vilna were very popular in our Jewish family. This was the city of the deep, limpid religious faith of the Vilna Gaon, the righteous convert; the city of the modern, free spirit of YIVO and the modern network of schools, the "smithy" of the Yiddish language. It was the stronghold of the Yiddish theater and its talents — Morevski, Vayslits, Samberg, Kamen and Shriftzetser. The great Yiddish cultural activists, like Dr. Tzemach Shabad and Dr. Wygodski, were living fountains of our cultural life. The children's journal *Grininke Beymelekh* ("Little Green Trees") was deeply rooted in my soul, and had also "grown up" in Vilna. But Vilna, the cultural crucible of Lithuanian Jewry, was crushed under armored fist of the Nazis.

Little by little, the truck slid onto the smooth, black asphalt of the city and cut through the streets at low speed. We were on a green bridge, over the turbid waves of the restless Vilna River that disappeared in a crooked arc underneath a green mountain. Dark houses, built in an old-fashioned style, stood like great noblemen. Not a "hair on their heads" had come to harm. Looking at them, it seemed to me as if there was no war in the world at all.

It was afternoon and there was lively movement in the streets. People of different ages, men and women, walked casually, talking loudly among themselves, laughing and window shopping. Somewhere on a street corner a radio announcer was rattling on, informing the world about the victories of Hitler's armies. But the crowds barely showed any reaction to the news and just continued on their way.

There was a Lithuanian policeman directing traffic at an intersection who looked like a mannequin with a wooden face. He was elegantly dressed, with white gloves and cuffs. Our driver stopped the truck and asked the policeman how to get to a garage where they could have the truck repaired. The policeman gave him directions in broken German. In the meantime, I searched the passers-by with my eyes. Maybe I would see a Jew.

Where had all the Jews gone to? I asked myself anxiously. Vilna had been a Jewish city after all. So where were they? Suddenly I felt dizzy and my eyes blurred. My heart beat fast. There they were. My brothers were walking in the gutter. A line of ten men, accompanied by a Lithuanian policeman, walked passed our truck, like common thieves and criminals, heads down, as if looking for their yesterdays and lost freedom.

With the stars of shame on their clothes, those ten men walked like the living dead. From time to time, one of them raised his head, and a poisonous, gall-bitter glance flew like an arrow at the crowd. It was the glance of a wounded eagle, whose wings were clipped, robbing it of its heavenly heights, a glance that cried out, "Look, world, how innocence itself bears your sins on its shoulders!" It was a look that warned, "World, you'll pay for my suffering." The policeman drove them brutally, grumbled something at them and they increased their pace.

After they left, the crowds on the pavement walked calmly, talking, laughing and continued on their way. This human indifference to our great misfortune scalded me, and deep in my heart I wished that they, too, would soon experience our pain for themselves.

The truck whined and moved off again, going in the indicated direction. We drove into the yard of a big metalworking factory, where it stopped. I left the truck, glanced in all directions, observed the workers and looked for Jews.

Opposite the factory building stood a low smithy. I went toward the fire, as if to light a cigarette. A blacksmith of medium height, solidly built, about 40 years old, stood hammering at the anvil. A second man sat by the furnace, turning the wheel of the ventilator. They were not wearing any tokens of shame on their work clothes, but from the looks we exchanged, I understood they were Jews.

Boldly I asked them in Yiddish: "Are you from Vilna?"

"Yes," both of them answered simultaneously, looking at me and breaking off from their work.

"And who are you?" the man at the wheel asked me.

"I'm from Grodno and now I'm going back home from Minsk in this truck," I replied. Two pairs of eyes stared at me suspiciously, quickly looking me up and down. Then the two of them exchanged ambiguous glances and returned to work.

The blacksmith turned the iron, beating it with his hammer, put the iron back into the fire and said: "How come, you're going with those black suits?" (The Dutchmen were dressed in black). I told them my whole sad history, as well as the situation in Minsk. Only then did they begin to trust me and started talking.

Words flew from their mouths like black crows, like afflictions from the Arabian Nights. Early mornings and days were bathed in Jewish blood, like the nights of St. Bartholomew. Dante's hell was a paradise compared to the suffering of Vilna's Jews.

In the first few months of the Brown Shirt and Lithuanian terror, the numbers were in the thousands, tens of thousands, and uncalculated "estimates" poured from their lips like drops of blood. "Actions," big and small, official and unofficial, had plucked out Vilna's Jews and cut them in four. Lithuanian nationalists and bandits felt firm ground under their feet. The happy hour of murdering and robbing Jews to their heart's content had finally arrived. The half-savage, stupid and aggressive Lithuanian hordes formed themselves into small Brown-Shirted gangs, and went through the city, catching Jews and slaughtering them in the Ponar. The thugs were sadly popular. Those people snatchers even outdid the SS in their sadism and "heroically" swam in rivers of Jewish blood.

The blacksmith grabbed a piece of iron from the fire, spat into his hand and started to bang ferociously with his hammer, as if he wanted to beat away his thoughts or pour his bitter heart onto the glowing iron. At last he hurled the iron away from him and was silent for a while. My head spun from this news. I sat down, lowered my eyes to the black soil on the ground, and remained silent.

He continued to speak. Short phrases fell from his mouth like hammer blows: "They chased us into the ghetto, gave us 15 minutes to pack, but in the end didn't let us take anything. Years of hard labor were gone with the wind. They herded a whole city of Jews together into narrow little streets. People are lying on top of each other, a prey to lice, epidemics and typhus. They packed the remaining Jews into the prisons, tortured them, without water or bread — young men, old people, women, little children — and in the end took them away to Ponar.

"And me? I remained alone, completely alone! Naked, hollow like the handle of this hammer." He turned his head away, wiped his wet eyes with his black hand and fell silent. I could not find any word of comfort for my unfortunate brother.

The blacksmith took me into the factory and led me to a Polish worker who stood at a turning-lathe, a middle-aged man with a pleasant face and kind eyes. "Speak to him," he said to me. "He's a good man and you can talk to him about everything. They help us a lot. Without them we'd die of hunger."

The Polish man gave me his calloused hand, asked me for news from Minsk and from the front, expressed his heartfelt pity for the situation of the Vilna Jews and told me the same story. Finally he added by way of justification: "We Poles in Vilna have got nothing to do with all of this. It's the Lithuanian nationalists and louts who are doing all these things, and we're also exposed to their harassment."

Probably he was a Leftist worker, because he added that the truth would be victorious and that "they" would still have to account for their bloody deeds. The simple words of an unknown friend deeply moved me and were like balm to my wounds. "We will never forget the friendship you are showing us in our great affliction," I answered him. Then I said good-bye and left.

The workday ended. The blacksmith suggested I come to the ghetto to sleep. The second man, who sat at the wheel, wanted to trade with me — an exchange of biscuits for my rolling tobacco. I gave him some rolling tobacco and told him to keep his biscuits.

Our truck was ready. The spring was repaired.

"Keep well, brother!" We pressed each other's hands and expressed a wish to see each other alive in better times.

Slowly the Vilna houses disappeared from my view, and soon the horizon covered the church steeples. I sat frozen in the car, my head heavy as lead, and kept hearing the blacksmith's words ringing in my ears — thousands, tens of thousands, prisons, slaughtered, Ponar — the Jews remained alone like the handle of the hammer without its head.

Well? And me? Where was I going? I stirred as if from a heavy dream and murmured to myself, "Maybe, maybe I am like the blacksmith's hammer-handle, too?"

The oak tree starts turning green later than all the other deciduous trees and even in late autumn it stands there, still green, as if its oak-tree strength was ready to continue its merciless fight for life. So these ancient oak trees stood, each in its appointed place at the side of the highway, toying with the autumn wind, not allowing a single leaf to fall from their green crowns. Birch trees, elder trees and aspen trees, half bare, shook their half-denuded branches toward each other, as if telling each other secrets: "Our end is near." The wind did not let the dead leaves rest, and took them up for a little dance. Then it carried them off far from their tree trunks.

The highway from Vilna to Grodno wound through vast, expansive fields, sparse bushes, wet meadows, small leafy woods and through long, dense forests, interrupted every 20 to 30 kilometers by large villages and small towns. Out in the fields were crude little villages and in the forest, concealed farmhouses. The autumn nights were cold, bright and dry. The sky was clear and wiped clean, without the least cloud — but try counting the stars...

The truck went through the wooded areas as fast as it could, as if afraid of what mysteries lay hidden in the mighty forest. But whenever there were little flames glowing in the night, it reduced its speed, feeling more at home when there was evidence of human habitation.

It was late when the truck drove noisily into the *shtetl* of Eshishok, located between Vilna and Grodno. It was a *shtetl* like many others on the Lithuanian border, where a few thousand Jews had lived, earning their crusts of bread through trade, skilled labor, gardening and the like. The shopkeepers had traded with the surrounding Lithuanian, White Russian and Polish peasants all their lives. The Jewish workmen built houses for them in the villages during the summer, had sewn coats of dowlas and boots for them in exchange for measures of grain or potatoes or a few zlotys in cash.

The Jewish peddlers and village merchants bought left-over flax, wool and pig's hair from the peasants or exchanged it for crockery, soap and fancy-goods. The *shtetl* had been lying in its centuries-old "slumber," steadily drawing its spiritual sustenance from Vilna, while at the same time boasting of its pedigree — 14 kilometers away was Raduń, where the great religious personality, the Chofetz Chaim — Rabbi Israel Meir HaCohen Kagan — lived and wrote his holy books.

The Jewish houses looked melancholy with their dark windows and no trace of life. Here and there bright electric lights from Christian windows cut through the darkness and sent their dagger-shafts into the gloomy Jewish houses. Somewhere a record player bellowed with all its might and half-drunk "liberated" Lithuanians danced an orgiastic dance, stamping their feet and clapping their hands, cutting through the silence with boisterous shouting and coarse guffawing.

The vehicle drove up to the Eshishok police station and stopped there for the night. I decided to go and visit my wife's sister and her family, to see if I could get some news about Frumke and Bashele. A Lithuanian man and young girl stood at the half-opened door of the police station. He noticed me when I clambered out of the car, looked me in the eye, bit his lip fiercely and asked me bitter as gall who I was and what I was doing there. I gave him an evasive, defiant answer and, to spite him, did it in Russian.

The young girl snapped at me angrily, "Are you still speaking that damn language?"

"Yes," I answered her with a dig. "In Russian it's easier for me to say what I want to say." They looked at me furiously and I enjoyed the notion that they wanted to bite me but couldn't.

Through the half-open door I scrutinized the police office. The wall was decorated with Hitler's big eagle, whose wings the loyal Lithuanians extended from one side to the other, and with sharp, twisted nails they'd stuck its feet to a globe on which they'd painted a black swastika. Beneath was an inscription in bold letters: "Long live Adolf Hitler."

Looking at the sacrilegious image of this bandit's insignia, it became unnecessary to ask the Jews in Eishishok for happy news. Though I was still under the influence of the "news" from Vilna, I tried to comfort myself, Maybe, just maybe it was a bit different here. And I went off to look for my relatives.

The night was silent, gloomy and melancholy, as if in a cemetery. The little Jewish houses stood like mourners, sunk in deep sadness, wrapped in the night. The little streets were barren. Shadows moved near the houses, talking quietly. There were no raised voices, a rarity in Jewish conversation.

"Good evening, my Jewish friends!" I called out. They turned to me with surprise and looked at my unfamiliar face. They groaned their "good evenings," surrounded me from all sides, looked me up and down and finally leapt at me with their questions. They particularly wanted to know where I was from and what news I had. I did not grow tired of answering each and every one of them. But I could not have been a good angel to the Jews in Eishishok in those sad days, because I considered it my duty to tell them the truth about Minsk and Vilna.

I cut them down with my news, and one after the other, their silhouettes slowly disappeared in the darkness. I held the last person back. "Tell me, what's your news here?" As if he just woke from a nap, he cast an absent-minded glance at me, was silent for a moment, then murmured, "Very bitter."

"But still. What's up?" I insisted. He turned his head to one side and quoted in an undertone: "Thou shalt not open thy mouth to Satan." ("*Al tiftach peh la Satan*"). And before I managed to answer him, he vanished.

I was surrounded by shadows in front of another house, and they fell on me with their questions. I answered every one, but could not get a definite word about their own plight from them. Their way of talking and their measured words made me realize that the air was electrified with the sense of disaster about to happen. They were struggling but could not run.

No one wanted to take me where I needed to go, which was a bit further out from the Jewish neighborhood. It was not out of malice, but they were afraid of their own shadows, of the danger that hung above their heads. Some of the Jews gave me directions: "Go right, past a birch wood fence, pass a well, avoid two houses…"

My hob-nailed shoes resounded strangely in the deserted streets. I never heard the sound of my own shoes as much as I did that evening in Eshishok. I came to my senses and walked confidently to the designated place. I stopped in front of a low little house, whose thatched roof was right by my head. I bent down and knocked at a dark little window, once, twice. The gray head of a man emerged from the darkness and he cautiously stayed at the closed window.

"Open up, my Jewish friend," I implored him. He opened up and looked at my face in fright. I called out the name of my friend Yaakov Michalovski. He cursed me: "Damn him! Such an impertinence, to knock at the window! Go to the devil! It's two houses further along the road," answered the Jew and shut the window in my face. I forgave him his curses, and I could understand their deathly fear. I knocked at the designated little window more cautiously now — once, twice, three times. But everything was quiet inside. I knocked again, a bit louder, and finally I called out in Yiddish: "Yankel, open up! It's me, Leibl, your brother-in-law!"

It was quiet for a second. Then there was a commotion of table and chairs and I heard voices, both happy and wailing ones, "Oh, Uncle Leibl! Uncle Leibl!" Faint candlelight cut through the darkness and shadows danced on the walls. I crawled through the window, and in those moments of joy my melancholy disappeared. They did not have any news about the fate of Frumke and Bashele, because they were so isolated. They set the table, and while we ate, we talked about local news.

The Lithuanians were preparing a general pogrom. That was no secret and it could happen at any moment. Yankel said these words quietly, stretched out on his bed, fully dressed; he smoked a cigar made of cheap rolling tobacco, and blew clouds of smoke that hovered in the faint glow. I broke the gloom and asked, "Why don't the children undress and go to bed?"

"This is the fourth night that we're sleeping fully dressed," the oldest child, a 12 year-old girl, answered.

"We're afraid to undress," said her younger sister, who was 10, finishing the sentence. Those children sat at the table. They were pale, and had black circles under their eyes from many sleepless nights. They looked right at me and, like grown-ups, listened attentively and with worry to every word I said. A nursing infant burst out crying in its mother's arms. She pressed her breast to the little baby's mouth, weeping silently, and now and then a tear fell from her bloodless cheeks onto the child's fluffy hair.

I could hardly get the food down. It was clear their fear was not exaggerated, that they had reason to worry about the future. It was obvious they felt their days were numbered, but they kept themselves alive with the great strength offered by hope. In my heart, I agreed that you could believe anything about the Lithuanian bandits, yet I also tried to console them.

"We're thinking of sending the children away to Raduń. It's a larger town, at least. Probably things won't be like this there," Yankel said.

"Absolutely," I fully endorsed them, "and it would be even better to send them to some non-Jewish acquaintances in the village." The candle flickered and went out. Hidden somewhere beneath the stove, a cricket chirped. Tired from the journey and battered by the news, I fell on the sofa and for a few hours, deep sleep freed me from my sad reflections.

The next morning I said good-bye to them, kissed them, hugged them, pressed their hands and expressed my dearest wish, which at that time could only be a dream, "To see each other alive!" And I went off to the truck.

The truck stood near the marketplace. Lithuanian policemen and village youths in high yellow boots ran wildly back and forth between the Jewish houses, hurrying the Jews to the marketplace for a head count. In all the ghettos, the Jews were counted frequently. In the big ghettos it was done by the Statistics Departments of the *Judenrat*; in the small *shtetls* it was done simply, in the marketplace, where they were counted like cattle. The Gestapo "kept an eye" on the Jews to ensure they did not disappear.

Dawn broke and the dreary and gray early morning covered the tin roofs with whitish autumn dew. Here and there policemen brutally beat victims to death with their rifle butts. As the Jews were beaten, they rolled about in the marketplace mud and did not even scream. Jewish children, 12 and 13-year-olds, with little faces like figs and wearing Stars of David on their torn clothes, looked like the fallen leaves of maple trees; they were forced to sweep the big marketplace and the gutters with brooms that were bigger than they were.

Pretending to be busy with the truck, I watched in deep inner turmoil as masses of unprotected people were being counted for perhaps the last time before their slaughter.

Later I learned that soon after I left, they made the *shtetl* "*Judenrein*" in one day. They drove their victims — 2,200 Jews — to mass graves. Both the SS and the Lithuanian police mocked the unfortunates sadistically, slaughtered them with machine guns and wooden posts, and covered the mass graves with lime. The soil on the graves stirred noticeably for several days after that and streams of blood gushed to the surface. That was the end of the Jews of Eshishok.

The truck continued to carry me toward my goal. The highway wound like a snake through the thickly wooded areas of the forest in their mysterious green density and drew us in. Then a cross appeared on the horizon, and after that the sloping roof of a church, then the church itself, and then a small town with little wooden houses, both new and half-ruined became visible. There was a "dead" marketplace, closed shops and gloomy Jews worked in the streets and on the highway with brooms and shovels.

Raduń, famous for the Chofetz Chaim's yeshiva, lay there as if in agony, without any traces of life. We stopped midway between Radun and Ostryna. The Dutchmen got out of the driver's cabin, took their milk churns and called me to come along to a nearby cottage to get some milk. We arrived at a village farmhouse, where a White Russian peasant woman, busy in the garden, moved toward us, looked at us and greeted us fearfully, then invited us in.

Little pigs rooted around the doorstep. A skinny child with a grubby face crawled around the courtyard. A shaggy dog on a chain barked impudently, struggling to get at us with its white teeth. The house smelled of leavened bread and peasant plenty. From the wall, Jesus looked wearily down at us. I thought a Star of David would have been more suitable for him than the inexpressive cross.

The peasant woman filled our containers with milk and gazed at us with mistrust.

"Ask her how she likes the new authorities." One of the drivers asked me to translate the question into Russian. I asked her with a sour expression. She looked at me confusedly, at my padded Red Army coat, at the Dutchmen, thought for a while, and at last said with a fake smile: "Not bad. For the time being it's alright."

"She's full of hope," I translated diplomatically.

"Have the Spaniards been here, and what did they want?" they asked.

"Yes, they were here," she answered more boldly. They had gestured with their hands in sign language and asked for "greasy stuff" — butter — as well as "cock-a doodle-doo" and "oink-oink" — that is chickens and pigs, in exchange for shirts, scarves, socks and the like.

I translated for the Dutchmen. "Ach!!" one of them grumbled. "They're everywhere, those guzzlers and defecators!"

He told me to tell the Christian woman that if the Spaniards were to return and ask for food, she should not give them anything. Obviously I translated this accurately and then added that she should also honor them with a big stick. The Christian woman burst out laughing and promised to act on the advice of the Dutch soldiers.

It was important for me to stop in Jeziory, 22 kilometers from Grodno, because I thought I would be able to find out exactly what had happened to Frumke and Bashele — if they were still alive and where they were living. That way I would not have to look suspicious, wandering around Grodno in vain,

Before getting into the truck, I said to the Dutchmen, "If you want to get some butter in exchange for cigarettes, we could do that in Jeziory. That's the small town by the big lake,"

"That's alright!" they agreed. "We'll stop there."

We stopped for a moment in Ostryna. Peasant women and pedestrians clambered up into the truck, along with a young German in a greatcoat with brown cuffs and a collar. I did not look in the bastard's direction. He, on the other hand, cast some curious, piercing glances at me.

Soon after that we stopped in Jeziory, I got off the truck quickly and ran to the Jewish streets. I stopped several young Jewish men and asked them about our good friend Sonia Kapulnik, who was a frequent visitor to our house before the war. I noticed her in the distance, ran to her and grabbed her hand. She looked at me for a moment and almost jumped. "Leibl, you're alive!"

As she came to her senses, she wiped her eyes and told me: "We heard you were dead, that someone saw you, shot dead on the highway to Minsk."

"Sonia, tell me quickly!" I said with difficulty. "Are Frumke and Bashele alive?"

I followed every movement of her lips with my eyes. "Yes!" was the happy reply.

"They're alive and they're living with your sister at 7 Napoleonska Street, because your home in Fershtot burned down."

"Keep well, Sonia!" I shouted and like a madman, ran back to truck. The two Dutchmen stood by the truck, and noticed my beaming face. One of them asked me: "Do you have news of your wife and child?"

"Yes, yes!" I shouted. "They're alive and waiting for me." I added apologetically that I could not get any butter. They exchanged glances and reassured me that they had gotten a quarter of a kilogram of butter by themselves.

The journey from Jeziory to Grodno was an hour of great joy for me, the joy of finding them alive, of myself being a gift for them because now I was on the proper track.

I had borne the guilt and pain through so many stormy days, avoiding the powerful zigzag rays of death. I crossed the deep abyss; I avoided brown snakes in forests and on highways. I burned with the Minsk ghetto, but had not been consumed. All of this gave me courage and energy for my continued struggle and kept alive the hope, deep in my heart, that we would survive.

When we arrived in Grodno, the truck stopped at the post office on Ozheshka Street. I bid farewell to my saviors from Minsk and briskly walked along Telegrafna Street, to 7 Napoleonska Street. The street was lively. Christian townspeople strolled at a leisurely pace along the main street, as they did five or 10 years earlier. I did not see any Jews. I held one hand over my eye, to disguise my face and to not attract the attention of the enemies and hooligans who filled the town to overflowing.

I found the house and ran up a few stone steps, stopping in front of a door painted bright yellow, with a paper Star of David glued to it. I rang the doorbell with all my might and could hear a child's footsteps coming to the door. Then the lock creaked and my sister's 14-year-old son stood before me.

"Mamma! Mamma! Come quick!" he shouted. "It's Uncle Leibl, Uncle Leibl!" A mixture of voices, kisses and salty tears sanctified the rapturous moment of seeing a living brother thought to be dead. When the turmoil calmed, my sister told me Frumke and Bashele were living on the next street and she was going to fetch them.

"But one must not surprise her intensely with such news," she added. "I'll tell her I received some news from you and the messenger is waiting in my house." A few moments later, Frumke was in the house, looking for the messenger in the room and she noticed me, stared at me for a moment and wildly fell into my arms. My 6-year-old daughter could not forgive me for kissing her mother for so long and ignoring her. She squealed loudly, like a steam engine, and I barely managed to persuade her to accept my apologies.

"You see, I've come back to you. It's true that I didn't run away from you for just a few days, as I had promised I would, but I was held up for a few months. That wasn't really my fault. It's the times we live in that prevented my return." I defended myself like a sinner in front of my wife and child. Tears choked my throat and stopped me from saying another word.

"What's the news? Tell me!"

"You'll see everything for yourself," Frumke answered as she wiped her eyes. "Our town is in ruins and we are in chains." There was not yet a ghetto in Grodno, but the Nazis fist constantly and mercilessly hammered on the heads of Grodno's Jews. According to the new German borders, the town now belonged to the Third Reich, and the border with White Russia was 50 kilometers further east, next to the small town of Szczuczyn. At first, this had fostered illusions among some Jews that in the Third Reich things would probably be different than elsewhere. But, in fact, bullying was doled out daily, like wormy peas. Jews were outside the law. Their lives and possessions were forfeit.

CHAPTER 8

Jewish Life under the Nazis in Grodno

The German police ruled the town with gangs of Polish hooligans and agitators, former members of the reactionary parties Endecja, Nara and OZON — who spread their arms to take advantage of the occasion to realize their dream of creating a *Judenrein* Poland. Their unjustified hostility toward the Jews had been accumulating for generations, a hostility fomented by the Polish governments of Pilsudski and Rydz-Śmigły. The Soviets took control in 1939, during which many of the Polish nationalists fled and after one and a half years of Soviet rule, Hitler's troops occupied the town. Polish antisemites began to work against the Jews. For the sake of accuracy, the majority of the Polish intelligentsia stood apart from these actions and passively watched the orgy of violence. Later they fell victim to the bloody sword themselves.

The majority of the thugs were simply having a good time. They were the uprooted petty bourgeois element. First they fought the Jewish intelligentsia. In the opening salvo, the first bloody cut, they "disappeared" the lawyers, advocates, teachers, accountants and other professionals. The Brown Shirts were cynical about it. They drove their cars through Grodno, stopped at the long lines in front of bread shops, and pretended to look for professionals to take to work. They took them away forever. Polish informers and agitators, lackeys of the Gestapo, constantly sent Soviet citizens — leftists and intellectuals who could not escape — to prison. That included the medical practitioner Shapranski, who was very popular and well-loved by the Jews.

It was difficult to recognize Grodno's streets. Almost half the town was rubble and ruined houses had crumbling, burned walls. The large Jewish quarter, where ordinary folk and poor people lived, was completely wiped out, as was the 300-year-old Great Synagogue, a historical treasure in Grodno.

Jews scratched in the ruins, digging up mugs, spoons, knives. Everything was a bonus for a wretched people stripped by fire of all their property. An unburned floor board, a rotten piece of masonry that the flames hadn't consumed — all that could be salvaged was dragged to newly-found homes shared with acquaintances and relatives, as everyone diligently prepared for winter.

Then the days of hunger began. Torn from their various professions, Jews worked as slaves paid with violence. Others — the luckier ones — could scrounge a bit of cooked food at their workplaces. Jews did all kinds of back-breaking labor. Right from the start, they were taken to dig potatoes, and had to crouch and crawl in the fields. They were bullied and forbidden to raise their heads or straighten their shoulders for entire days. Those who raised their heads, even a little, were shot on the spot.

The Jewish workforce was used to clear forest areas; to level mountains; to demolish condemned buildings in the town; to work on sewage systems and similar projects that would have taken years and lots of money to complete. The Jews were put to work with a fierce determination, giving the "town fathers" the opportunity to take advantage of a golden moment to rebuild and modernize their infrastructure with Jewish slave labor.

Inexperienced youths did dangerous jobs, like gathering ammunition and taking hand grenades apart, and many of them paid with their lives. They collected the damaged war machinery, cannon and tanks from the highways, took them apart and loaded them onto wagons that brought it all to the furnaces for melting down. They washed locomotives and wagons and served the starving Russian prisoners who were sick with typhus. They collected bricks and gravel from around the town and tore down walls that were hardly stable. Such was the work of the slave brigades, who, starving, were forced to exert themselves to the limit.

Then the Germans ordered the *Judenrat* to be established. Its main tasks were supposed to supply German workplaces with slave laborers, and to siphon off astronomically high contributions of money, gold and other valuables from the Jewish population. All Jews had to pay these contributions and the *Judenrat* assessed everyone according to a sliding scale, and even the poor were not spared payment of these "fines".

The *Judenrat* had a Department of Requisitioning with very precise evidence of which Jew had the best pillows or beds and other material goods. Every day the *Judenrat* received ordinances from different German departments ordering them to supply bedding, furniture, crockery, electrical appliances, manufactured goods, leather and the like. The Germans rejected nothing. They demanded everything: prams, medical instruments. (Cameras and radios had been forbidden from the beginning — on pain of death). The Gestapo, on the other hand, was very "choosy." They demanded "only" nicely polished furniture, good mattresses, material for making suits, down-filled duvets, finely-stitched curtains, perfumes, toilet soap and other "little somethings" — like liquor, raisins, real coffee, cocoa, sardines and pure alcohol. This all had to be delivered punctually, at the appointed time, and was the *Judenrat's* "political and economic program."

One looked for ways to ease the hunger assaulting every Jewish household. Rich people buried their fortunes, so they would not fall into the hands of the Brown Shirts. The poor people's tongues hung out of their mouths from hunger. They "speculated," selling the last shirt, sheet and jacket they owned to non-Jews for a morsel of bread, flour or bit of cooking fat.

The *Judenrat* set up a soup kitchen in the Great Synagogue. People stood in long lines, among them a few intellectuals turned laborers. Each of the hungry received a little watery cabbage soup and 30 grams of bread for lunch.

The non-Jews in town took the opportunity to acquire the last few poor Jewish possessions by "moral means" — that is by paying for them. Others did it by force. They lured their victims to their houses, took their last shirts or dresses, hit them, threw them out and perhaps even threatened to report them to the Gestapo for speculating.

Hunger stopped at the window of our little house. We had to think of something to chase it away. I did not have any desire to lend a helping hand to drive Hitler's war machine and did not reply to any of the *Judenrat's* demands. Instead, I went to work at the Jewish hospital, which, after the bombings, was in ruins, with smashed walls, shattered windows and broken doors.

With less than 100 beds, it served a population of more than 20,000 people. One has to pay tribute to the medical staff, mostly the doctors who, like loyal sailors on a sinking ship, continuously helped the population. No one forced them to do what they did. They were driven by adrenaline in those dangerous days. They brought help to our unfortunate brothers during the last months of their lives and were with the people until the very last moment.

May the names of Doctors Finkel, Bloimshtein, Suchovlianski, Naiman and Lipnik, and medical practitioners Yonas and Reizer forever remain in our memory.

CHAPTER 9

News and Rumors

On a sunny autumn day, a truck drove up to the hospital and several metalworkers carried Avrom Labdenz in on a stretcher. He had been shot.

They lowered the stretcher to the stone floor in the corridor. Then several apples fell from the dead man's chest. The blood-soaked apples rolled about on the floor, leaving crooked red lines in their wake. The young men were disoriented and told us that hunger tormented them. "We restrained ourselves, but he," they said, pointing to the dead man, "could not restrain himself. He left the workshop, went to the apple tree, jumped up, caught a branch and shook off a few apples. For that, the guard put a bullet in his belly."

They fell silent, looked at their friend and the doctor on duty. A few rays of sun sneaked into the dark corridor, lighting up the dead man's face, sharpening his cheekbones and nose, making them more visible. The eyes of the dead man were open, as if in the last tense moments of his life he had not wanted to be deprived of blue skies and sunshine.

Often Jews who were run over or maimed were brought in. Jews were forbidden by law to walk on the pavements, only in the cobblestone gutters. That gave many Brown Shirt drivers the opportunity to play a game with their victims, "unintentionally" knocking them down. Every day the morgue was full of those who were murdered. The hospital wards were filled with people who had fractured skulls, broken arms, broken legs and crushed ribs. There was no gauze or bandages. Old shirts and rolls of paper were used instead.

The authorities did not dispense medicine, so we made do with emergency supplies leftover from the Soviets, and looked for sources in town where we could buy medicine on the black market.

One day a 40-year-old woman who had been stabbed was brought to the hospital. Her clothes were soaked with blood. I helped lay her down on the table and pulled her bloody clothes off. She had several deep knife wounds around her heart. Her mind was no longer clear, and she was babbling. Her thin ribs protruded from her skinny sides like little hoops. Rivulets of brown blood seeped from her wounds. She could not hold her head straight, emitted a rattling sound and clung to my hand with her skinny, sticky fingers. Those who brought her to the hospital said a Polish woman attacked her, cursed her and finally shouted, "You have no rights today!" then stabbed her several times. At that moment it was not important to know who this non-Jewish woman was and why she had done this.

The last autumn days of 1941 were bleak and muddy. The sky moved above our heads, gloomy and tearful, spraying a fine drizzle. A biting cold permeated our clothes, licked our bodies and chilled our blood. The weather crept into our bones, as if making common cause with the enemy. During one cold night, it seemed the entire hospital staff was sitting in the corridor at the warm stove, deeply engrossed in a discussion about "How long can this last?"

Suddenly, the hospital doorbell rang impatiently. The doorman opened the door, and two Polish youths came in, former pupils at the Polish state grammar school. They looked into everyone's face impertinently and demanded that we hand over the son of Kleinbart, the hospital's cook. He had been a machinist and member of the factory committee at the town's water works during the time of the Soviets.

He was hiding in the hospital and, knowing that they came for him, disappeared in time through a side door. One of the former pupils had a whip in his sleeve and sniffed out nooks and crannies like a dog. The doctor on duty (Suchovlianski) explained to our "guests" that this was a hospital for the sick, not for anyone else. They looked fiercely at the doctor, whispered something between them and left.

One day I discovered a ruined little house near the hospital and decided to move us in. I filled the holes in the wall and the broken window frames with clay. I replaced glass panes with thin plywood, cutting some "portholes" to let in some light. I borrowed a bed and little table from acquaintances and prepared for winter. Frumke sold some of our clothes and got some potatoes, bread and a bit of flour. Every day I would bring home a small bag of wood shavings. Little by little, we stored for the whole winter. Bashele played with the autumn blossoms in the abandoned garden, always asking us for some bread, and when she had some, ran around happily in the garden.

We soon repaired the damaged hospital. Despite our empty stomachs, we bricklayers, painters, metalworkers and carpenters rushed to get the work done. There was a sense of responsibility to the community ingrained in us and even the artisans found consolation in socially useful work that benefited their tormented brothers.

The broken windowpanes were replaced with plywood, so the biting wind did not have as much power and patients were no longer blue from the cold. Tirelessly, the nurses cared for the patients, easing their wounds with kind words, caresses, or a bit of medicine. The ever-friendly medical practitioner Yonas used his sense of humor to chase away patients' melancholy moods with jokes. In serious moments, he admitted he had two rifles hidden in the cellar and that as soon as "they" started to retreat, we would accompany them with buckshot dumplings.

All our conversations were about news from the front. Victory communiqués were plastered on the walls, informing people of the heroic battles and the occupied territories of the Soviet Union. At the same time, the Nazis and their collaborators conducted a savage Jew-baiting propaganda campaign, boosted by disgusting antisemitic caricatures in the style of Streicher and Goebbels.

The civilian population was besieged and isolated. Apart from the official Nazi press that was full of lies, there was no connection with the outside world. Listening to the radio was punishable by death and they were confiscated at the beginning of the occupation. Careful people and great risk-takers hid their radios in a cellar, an attic or field. From time to time they lent an ear to the world. But by the time the news made it to us, it would be hazy, crisis-laden, rumor-filled, overspiced, full of weird stories and very cheerful.

The mouth-to-ear telegraph — or the "telegraph agency JWILT," was an acronym for "Jews want it like this," — every Jew added "something extra" so that by the time the news came to the tenth Jew, it would be dangerously exaggerated. Even the names of towns were mixed up. When the Nazis were defeated in Libya, a friend came to me with great joy, because he heard that "they" had been chased out of Lida (100 kilometers away). They often changed Berlin to Lublin, and the names of White Russian towns at the distant front to towns nearby.

People revived themselves with smelling salts and longed for the enemies downfall. They repeated news cautiously, to good friends and acquaintances, and while doing so, confirmed it came from good sources. All these canards boosted hope and reinforced the illusion that "they" would probably retreat without their hats and would forget about us. We would survive and live to joyfully tell the tale.

But there were no significant defeats of the Brown Shirts. The bandit march of Hitler's armies continued and from hour to hour, the Brown Shirt semi-circle around Moscow was tightened.

Often we got the sad news of Hitler's machinations in neighboring *shtetlach*. Marching to the front, the Brown Shirts would murder whole Jewish communities with varying methods. They burned Jews in their houses of study, or made the whole *shtetl* run the gauntlet down one narrow passageway, beat them to death with fence posts, or gathered the entire Jewish population in an open field, told them to run, and then shot them. This was supposed to "harden" young soldiers who never experienced a "military campaign," and had not been immersed in human blood. They practiced on Jewish mothers, fathers and children, hardening their hearts for their "heroic" battles.

Soon people said they had good sources who told them it would soon be time to move to the ghetto being created in a designated area. As always, the Jews had contrary opinions about whether or not there would be ghettos in the Third Reich. Then several "authorized" Jews murmured about the ghetto. This was unpleasant news, though the Jews in Grodno had not yet tasted ghetto life.

It did not bode well. Being isolated from the world already gave rise to various gloomy thoughts, which pecked at our brains like hungry crows. We were tormented by wondering how we would live and earn our crusts of bread. How would we move our few bags and bundles from here to there?

At the time Grodno's Jews could not have fathomed that the establishment of the ghetto was a step toward Hitler's goal of annihilating us, that they would put us there all together, fenced in, under the constant eye of the Brown Shirts, who would be able to take us at any moment and transport us to death factories or mass shootings. Again, people responded, as usual, with a "Hmm" or a "Ha!" and a "Ho-Hum" — they assumed that it was just that the Germans didn't want us doing business or going to to our non-Jewish neighbors.

From the beginning, it seemed strange and outrageous that the Germans could imprison tens of thousands of people behind barbed wire. All the talk created chaos and made our lives even more bitter. People feverishly prepared for the new plague, by trying to supply themselves with food.

Once again, people sold what they could — a spare jacket, a shirt, a pillow, furniture, crockery — anything that one could exchange for food was sold for next to nothing. Cunning peasants and townspeople understood this golden opportunity to haggle to get the fruit of many years' labor from the Jews for a pittance. Cheerful peasants went home with wagons loaded with Jewish possessions, singing drunkenly, as if it was a good day at the market.

The urban element was choosier and did not buy or exchange just anything. They demanded new suits, manufactured goods, good bed linens, modern shoes, jewelry, gold and so forth. Many of them walked around on weekdays, dressed like dandies, and constantly grabbed golden fox furs from the Jews. Others would speak plain words, cuttingly, coldly and cynically, "You'd better sell this to us. You won't need it any longer."

There were also various "friends" who went to their Jewish acquaintances and implored them to entrust them with their poor possessions — they would be returned after the war. They claimed they had no thought other than the Jews' well being. They were "friends" with a far-sighted outlook, who understood Hitler's policies very well and had a yen for an inheritance. There were also genuine friends, who had good intentions, but there were, unfortunately, very few of them.

CHAPTER 10

Moving into the Ghetto

As if it fit the troubled times, inclement weather hit us. Fiercely cold days took turns with one another. Evil winds howled like packs of wolves and did battle with the plywood "windowpanes." Our faces were slapped with cold raindrops that pushed their way through our clothes to our bodies. The gray, ragged sky hung over our heads like a curse, as if about to fall. When we looked through the hospital windows, we noticed that on the other side of the railway, Jewish brigades were feverishly setting up a barbed-wire fence that surrounded the outskirts of the Słobodka suburbs.

Using clubs, the Polish taskmasters harassed the Jews. They dug holes, erecting posts, put up wires, and little by little, a ghetto was established. On the evening of the last day of October 1941, the weather got worse. The furiously cold wind subsided and heavy, stinging snow fell like chunks of cotton wool, covering the thick mud beneath our feet in white down. This guest, "Uncle Snow," was neither valued nor welcome. He arrived too early, presaging a long winter to come. The next day, November 1, we were forced to move into the ghetto.

I constantly wracked my brains trying to figure out how to get our few poor possessions behind the wire, for the German order specifically said we had to be in the ghetto with everything we were bringing by noon. No hired or non-Jewish transportation was permitted.

How would I save my two sacks of potatoes and half a sack of flour? We had some pots, a few old clothes, a small table, a chair. My head felt like it was going to explode, but I could not figure out a solution. That night, I was so frustrated, that I got out of bed and went into the courtyard. The snow was still falling, making the white blanket still thicker. The snowy whiteness refreshed my nerves a little and reminded me of past good times playing in the snow and going for sleigh rides.

"Oh, you fool, you great fool!" I thought, and slapped myself in the forehead. I flung myself at the wooden fence, tore out a plank and in no time had a sled ready. I dragged it into the house, woke my wife and showed her my idea. She laughed with joy and I went to sleep happy. My sleep was sweet and sound that final night, when we were still "equal" citizens of Grodno. The next day we moved to the ghetto, the same kind of ghetto that confined our great-grandfathers during the Middle Ages.

Before dawn we stood harnessed to our sled, waiting for permission to set out for the ghetto. Most of the streets were blocked off and heavily guarded by gendarmes and Polish policemen. The gendarmes carried machine guns and wore steel helmets, pulled well down on their heads, as if it were a major military operation. Under the helmets, serpent-like eyes glared at us. The Polish police, on the other hand, were armed with "more humane" weapons — sticks and whips — and were attired in Hitlerian fashion, namely in black, and they wore — for the "feast" — white gloves.

Soon the streets were opened and, like an avalanche, Jews pushed from every side in the direction of the two ghettoes. We were swept up by the powerful stream and marched toward Ghetto No. 1, the one intended for qualified professionals. Our heavy sled sank deeply into the snow, which was trampled, black and muddy. With superhuman effort, I slowly dragged it along. A journey of almost a kilometer lay ahead of us. With our last strength, we managed to drag ourselves near the ghetto entrance. There was an intense crush in "the Butcher's Street," a narrow alley that served as an entrance and people crawled over each other like ants.

In the nearby square, there were mountains of furniture, bundles of bed linens, food and other things. The crowd was thrust forward in a frightening manner while trying to get into the "good" ghetto, Ghetto No. 1, as quickly as possible. Gendarmes checked papers in a relaxed fashion, felt the bundles, put the better furniture and clothes to one side, and at last let the almost naked "lucky ones" through the gate.

We had no time to waste and decided to go to Ghetto No. 2 in Slobodka, the one intended for non-qualified Jews. (The ghetto covered an area of about 500 x 800 meters, two-thirds consisting of arable fields. It was on the eastern edge of Grodno and included the small village of Pavilanke). The road was muddy and our sled stuck to the mud. The wires of the sled's harness bit deeply into my flesh. Rivulets of sweat ran down my face, smeared with mud, but I continued carrying my yoke with superhuman effort. I stopped for a minute to gulp some cold air and marched a few more steps forward.

Everyone around us was moving. Families with kith and kin carried their few poor possessions on their backs. Laden from head to toe with bags, bundles, crockery and furniture, an entire town retreated behind the wire, dragging overloaded prams piled high with beds and cupboards. Relatives carried sick people on their shoulders through the muddy streets. Like lunatics, people harnessed themselves to their featherbeds and dragged themselves toward the ghetto. The poor man carried his bag of sorrows, rags and blackened pots. The wealthy man carried his last few clothes, and was robbed at the ghetto gate.

The pavements, balconies and windows were loaded with curious "fellow citizens." There were many Poles who did not conceal their joy and laughed heartily in the midst of the gloom. The Polish police, once again, maintained order in "exemplary" fashion, by beating people black and blue with their truncheons, feeling their bundles and stuffing the things they took into their wallets and coat pockets. The gendarmes were more tactful, demanding only leather, manufactured goods and gold.

We managed to get back to the apartment to make a second journey with our sled and then we became citizens of the ghetto. We needed to get some rest. My hands and sides were cut by the harness and I could barely lift my feet — they felt as if they were broken.

We immediately needed to find a place to live. It became dark quickly and soon it was pitch-black. We headed to the village and barely managed to get there in the murky night. It was abandoned by the peasants, who were evacuated on the same day to Jewish houses. I touched the little door of a cottage in the darkness, opened it and we found ourselves standing in a small empty peasant house with a clay floor.

"Do you like this palace?" I asked Frumke. She did not answer, and lowered herself to the floor, exhausted. We fell soundly asleep, as if struck dead on the hard clay floor. When we woke, a gray ghetto day gazed inside through the small window and summoned us outside to look at Hitler's "Jewish kingdom." The ghetto was in an area full of clay and mud. Jews were endlessly churning up the mud, as they walked back and forth like ants in an anthill. They were still looking for places to lay their heads. People shared their piece of floor and a corner of their beds — each according to his social position and morality.

Jews still carried heavy bundles, groaned and muttered among themselves. "I wouldn't do anything else to them, but chase us into a different ghetto every month."

The ghetto lay behind a high, thick wire fence with a single gate, where a gendarme stood with a Jewish policeman. Like mushrooms after rain, young men with truncheons appeared, recruited by the *Judenrat*. They had blue ribbons on their caps and armbands on their sleeves. With their sergeants, officers and police chiefs, they kept order with a firm hand. Initially considered "Purim police," they slowly turned into the lackeys of the gendarmes and later, when the ghetto was liquidated, were traitors to the people and faithful servants of the Gestapo. The people could "smell" them and hated them, not because Jews did not like order, but because people sensed that they were synonymous with Hitler's rule.

Like faithful dogs, they stood at the barrier, standing guard and taking money to turn a blind eye to every Jew smuggling in a pound of potatoes, grain, flour or other vital commodity. For them, the gate was a source of blackmail, bribes and a life of comfort. They wallowed in prosperity at the expense of their hungry brothers.

In other cities, ghetto militia understood the great disaster and allowed people to smuggle in weapons; later they helped youths escape to the forests. Some of them died true heroes and others were honorable partisans.

People hated the *Judenrat* and its functionaries — bureaucrats who were like a plague foisted on the body of the people and who had a twisted and cowardly relationship to the people's interests. At the top were semi-intellectuals and assimilationists. The general purpose of these men was to force others into line. They demanded loyalty, believing and waiting — maybe, maybe... But the authorities were a toy in the hands of the Gestapo and an instrument for luring the unfortunates to Treblinka and Auschwitz.

Our work at the hospital was wasted, because once we were put into the ghettoes, the order came to transfer the hospital. We found the means to quickly set up a hospital for patients with contagious diseases, because the overcrowding, dirt and terrible living conditions were causing typhus to spread and we had to make every effort to stop it.

Slowly we settled into ghetto conditions and adapted to our new way of life. The inhabitants of the ghetto demonstrated wonderful creative energy and enterprise, illegally developing, under draconian measures, an entire light industry, which also catered to "export." People produced artificial honey, soap, liquor, soft leather, oil, starch, molasses, sweets, all sorts of cereals, and tobacco — cut by hand and wrapped into packets.

All of this was produced by a primitive underground system. When "guests" suddenly appeared in the ghetto, the contraband had to disappear. Raw materials were smuggled in by various means, even in officially distributed supplies, hidden beneath wood or potatoes. The carters had hiding-places in their wagons and used sanitation barrels — which were removed from the ghetto to be emptied — equipped with inner partitions used to smuggle food.

Jews earned their crusts of bread to the annoyance and surprise of their enemies, who expected them to die of hunger in the ghetto. Instead, the Jews were providing food to their neighbors! The Jews' inexhaustible creative energy was admirable. Were our ghetto great-grandfathers, who sold the finest muslins and the loveliest silks, still in our blood? Was the heroic struggle to survive throughout the centuries, which hardened our willpower, a factor in our creativity and helping us tolerate ghetto conditions?

This factor, a specifically Jewish one, and a positive aspect of our hard ghetto life, could not have existed in another people! Put in our place, other nationalities would have died of hunger within the first few months.

Hidden deep within the cellars, little electric mills ground grain and provided flour to black-market bakers who sold it for a high price. A refugee from Lodz turned a shed near our house into a coffee factory. Every night he roasted 200 kilograms of coffee beans in a special oven. Then he ground the beans in a medieval hand-mill and delivered coffee to ghetto residents and townspeople.

Despite the economic activity, most of the ghetto residents lived in dire poverty and waited for a bit of bread. Each morning, throngs of Jewish workers left the ghetto to perform forced labor in the town. They did all kinds of back-breaking labor, and suffered much agony at the hands of their slave-drivers. Every night they came home exhausted, dragging themselves along. Often they were bruised and bloody, and had broken bones. They were carried on the arms of their fellow workers. The more fortunate smuggled in a bit of wood, a few kilos of potatoes, a piece of fat, all cleverly concealed.

The women did not sit with their hands folded. They strained their brains thinking about how to get some bread and help their husbands make a living. They had certificates that said they were "seamstresses," and would leave the ghetto, to return with bags of potatoes, peas, or flour — it depended on which gendarme stood at the gate.

If "Grandma" stood there (an old, lazy gendarme), it was not too bad. He was too lazy to get up, to feel and check, and usually pretended not to see. But when "Monkey" or "Storm" were on guard, it was bad. They seized "merchandise" and gave people beatings into the bargain.

CHAPTER 11

Jewish Youth in the Ghetto

The disaster was terrible for our young people. Despite everything, they were beginning to blossom in their youthful exuberance, just before they died by violence. If the old people had lost one heaven, the young lost all seven. A highly cultured and educated young generation was growing up, for whom, a year and a half before the war the Soviet authorities had opened the doors of life. They allowed young people to march to the "top of the mountain" with heads held high. All the schools, institutions and departments formerly barred to Jewish youth were fully open. There was even a conservatory, where our youngsters demonstrated their budding musical talents.

Day and night, we were often deafened by those young people, free as birds, as the sounds of their singing and balalaika playing rang through the alleys and main streets of Grodno. It was like a joyful cry of vengeance for the stolen years of their youth and the oppression of their nation. At sports competitions and youth festivals they blossomed proudly, courageously and charmingly. Each and every one had dreams — to become an engineer, a pilot, a seaman, an engine driver.

The war mercilessly destroyed all these dreams and ruined their youth. They were consigned once again to a lower, inferior national level, and they suffered under the Brown Shirt terror no less than the grown-ups. They understood the depths of their misfortune — they were like proud eagles locked in a cage, waiting for the "something" that was surely bound to happen. They were the ghetto's news carriers. They picked up a bit of good news somewhere and quickly brought it to the ghetto, explained it in detail, commented on it, drew a map on the palms of their hands and made it clear to the grown-ups that "this" was only a question of a few months, until "they" retreated. In such holy moments of reverie, one could forget the Yellow Star, the ghetto, the hunger and the beatings, just for a while, and pretend to be floating in the air, in some platonic dream.

Just like the grown-ups, from the age of 14 boys bore the heavy burden of forced labor. Dressed in rags and split shoes, they left from the ghetto gate, each day hoping to hear the "right news" and to smuggle something back in. The younger children performed miracles, sneaking out of the ghetto, taking off their yellow stars. They dealt in potatoes, grain, flour and milk, hurling them through the wires as quickly as devils and disappearing right under the noses of the Jewish policeman.

Others of the same age were "merchants" on a smaller scale, carrying their little shops around in their arms, calling out their wares in their little voices: cigarettes, matches, saccharine, cigarette paper and the like. The very small children played new, modern games like "At the Gate." The children imitated the gendarmes, policemen, the Jewish women carrying a few potatoes. They would imitate the gendarme beating her with his stick, as he shouted "Cursed Jew, you're swindling!"

In the evenings, they gathered in the dark corridors of the barracks and recalled the good times at school and the cinema, when they freely walked the streets, and remembered the river, the forests — and groaned just like the grown-ups. Through the night, we heard them singing the haunting tune of the popular ghetto song, written by an unknown, gifted folk poet:

> It was a gloomy day,
> The fall of the first snows,
> When they chased all the Jews
> Into the two ghettos.
>
> Refrain:
> Woe to the Jews,
> Who have no home,
> Woe to the Jews,
> Who have no freedom,

Have remained wretched, have nowhere to roam,
Woe to the Jews,
Wretched as a stone.

We came to the barbed wire,
They commanded us to bide,
Took away our prized possessions
And ordered us inside.

— Refrain —

Four families in every room,
Eight people to a bed packed tight
And the housewives in the kitchen
Fighting day and night.

— Refrain —

CHAPTER 12

Aktionen in the Ghetto

There was no place to hide from winter's heavy snows and severe frost. There was no wood or other fuel. Wherever there were wooden fence boards or little trees, people removed them like blood vessels from meat. Century-old trees in the ghetto were dug up by the roots. Sheds and other abandoned wooden buildings disappeared overnight. Sometimes people would attack a small abandoned wooden house in broad daylight like hungry wolves, and "devour" it in no time. But that hardly helped drive away the vicious cold.

Like winter's freezing temperatures, the *Führer*'s speeches became more savage by the day. He bawled through the radio speakers, threatening the world with a bitter end. Every speech was well-seasoned with deadly antisemitic poison and bilious Jew-baiting, ordering the Jews not to laugh or suffer illusions.

The *Führer* felt such confidence in his prophetic powers that one Wednesday, on the radio, in broad daylight, he declared that during the next 48 hours events of great historical significance would take place that would have a powerful effect on the outcome of the war. But 48 hours passed and then another 48 hours passed and nothing terrible happened. On the contrary, the Germans suffered ever fiercer blows near Moscow. "Well," people remarked to one another, "This idiot may well be a *Führer*, if he's got such oxen for a people."

Snowflakes like salt crystals fell ceaselessly, stung our faces and shimmered before our eyes like diamonds. The *Führer* talked on, "It is 200 years since we have had such a frost in winter. Our soldiers are demonstrating their mighty strength and beating the enemy. We did not desire this war. This war was forced on us by the world plutocracy and by the Jews, and they will have their war."

After such speeches, the gendarmes wielded their sticks more zealously, and Jews would come home from work beaten black and blue. On the other hand, the speeches "comforted" us; they meant that the dog was grinding his teeth — a sign he was receiving blows, or so people told one another, and accepted their beatings with love, knowing that somewhere an avenging hand was at work.

One winter morning I left our little house, and headed to the ghetto hospital to get some news. The sun's cold rays stung my eyes and the sun painted the white snowy fields in brilliant colors, glittering brightly in my eyes. Near the barbed wire, on the other side of the ghetto fence, heavily laden sleighs squeaked in the deep snow.

I looked to see what was on the other side of the fence and froze. Several big sledges were laden with naked human corpses and moved slowly toward the Slavic cemetery. There were many corpses, piled like logs on the low, wide sledges. Here and there an arm or a leg dragged behind, drawing a deep line in the snow. The corpses' completely shaven heads, shook powerlessly back and forth, as if empathizing with some sad tale. A gendarme guarded 10 pale prisoners of war who carried shovels and were going to bury their comrades.

I shook myself, as if emerging from a nightmare, and called Fruma, shouting: "Look, on the other side of the fence!" She watched the bizarre, gruesome scene for a while, turned white as chalk and ran, weeping, back into the house.

After that, sledges laden with dead prisoners of war, withered by typhus and hunger, frequently passed our house, The ghetto Jews, who worked among the prisoners and quietly shared their last bit of bread with them, told us that they were also loading men still alive with the corpses, since the Germans forced them to throw their comrades in among the dead. Those people were buried alive.

One evening they smuggled one of the dying men, a candidate for the mass grave, out of the prisoners' camp, and hid him among rags in a wagon. They brought him to the ghetto hospital where the doctors tried hard to save him. They did not leave his bedside and eventually got him on his feet again. He was a lieutenant, an airman in the Red Army, whose name was Lifshits. Evil tongues came to know this and carried the news to the Gestapo.

Instantly the Gestapo appeared in the ghetto, arrested their victim and took him off to their headquarters for an investigation. Lifshits probably had little desire to converse with them and vanished through an open window. Following this episode, several doctors fled the ghetto or hid themselves very well.

From the start, the Poles morally capitulated to the enemy. Most of them dreamed that Hitler would rebuild Poland for them, but then became disappointed in the "Brown Messiah" and even turned their noses up. At the beginning of 1942, a gendarme and a Polish policeman stopped a suspicious wagon at the edge of town and wanted to search it. The wagon driver, a Pole, drew a pistol, killed the gendarme, badly injured the policeman and disappeared. The Gestapo, unable to capture the gunman, announced publicly that if he were not handed over within three days, the Polish population would be held responsible.

As usual, the Gestapo kept their promise. When the deadline came and the criminal wasn't handed over, the Gestapo arrested 100 Poles from the intelligentsia. This did not please our fellow citizens. What did the Germans mean by seizing Poles and arresting them? — especially doctors, lawyers, teachers and priests. They were not Jews, after all, and hoped this was probably just intimidation and that those taken would be set free.

On the evening of the third day the Gestapo lined up 100 prisoners in the courtyard and ordered every fourth man to step out of the line. They took these 25 men out of the town and killed them with a machine gun. The others were released. After this episode, the Poles lowered their voices a bit and noticed their redeemer had claws.

From time to time the town's rationing department threw a few tons of rotten potatoes into the ghetto, as well as turnips, horse meat and, once, even pork. It was only when the veterinarian in the slaughterhouse found a pig to be unhealthy that its meat was transferred to the ghetto. The horse meat was worse. In most cases it came from worn-out horses whose hides were taken to the leather factory, while the meat was buried in pots in the ghetto. A piece of horse meat was difficult to cook and even after many hours over the fire, it remained tough and sinewy. My wife, poor thing, struggled hard with horse meat until she thought of making it into meatballs. Then it was fine. We also poured strong horseradish over the "meatballs" to banish the smell of horse, and swallowed them quickly. We made kugel, out of the rotten potatoes, and that formed an important part of our diet.

Around Pesach, the sun crept out and melted the thick crust of ice on the ground. The sun caressed us, warmed us and, as always in the spring, announced new life. The ghetto lay in a river of water that descended from the surrounding mountains. The Jews built a little bridge out of bricks, threw stones in the water, and leapt adroitly from stone to stone, trying to figure out how to return to their little houses and stay dry. The water soon receded, and left behind a deep, thick mud that squelched beneath our feet.

Soon the field in the ghetto lay bare, damp and warm, yearning for a skilful farmer's hands. People were looking for better ways to fight hunger. So Jewish gardeners gathered, went to the field, felt the soil, rubbed it between their fingers, measured its length and width with their steps, took ploughs out to the field, and soon sharp steel cut the bare earth. The Jews walked behind the plows with their sleeves rolled up, controlling the blade in the soil, just as they had in their own fields in times of peace. They called out joyfully to one another and probably forgot they were in the ghetto in the spring of 1942.

I watched those healthy Jewish farmers and was overcome by a strong desire to follow their example. "Much better than working for Hitler," I told myself, and tilled a piece of land next to our house. In the course of one day I prepared 30 patches. I turned the earth over and combed it with a rake, until the patches shone symmetrically like beautiful prisms. Soon I had a garden producing all sorts of good things: radishes, cucumbers, beets, tomatoes and so forth. We began living a much better way. For the first time in my life I realized how good it was to enter into "partnership" with the earth.

Along with the sunny days, horrible news arrived from neighboring provinces. It told of mass slaughters and killings of whole or part of Jewish populations in different towns. In the first days of May, several people came running from Lida and gave us details of the gruesome slaughter there. Soon more news arrived, all about destroyed *shtetls* and plundered Jewish goods. In the summer of 1942, many larger and smaller Jewish settlements in western White Russia were completely wiped out.

Where we were living, in the Third Reich, people thought it probably would not be that way. It was the Third Reich after all! So people twiddled their thumbs and deceived themselves. A Jew who fled Warsaw turned up in our ghetto. In great secrecy he told us that many Warsaw Jews were being taken away somewhere, as if for work. People did not yet know exactly where they were being taken, but surmised that there was nothing good going on.

We received the news with considerable skepticism. Our healthy common sense could not digest the naked truth, or we were not psychologically prepared for such a great catastrophe. We simply could not believe that the Nazis' cruelty would ever include total annihilation.

Hitler's, Goebbels' and Goering's speeches were considered the barking of dogs, the antisemitic "oil" for the wheels of war, and people still couldn't believe that the murderers meant what they said in their speeches.

"They won't do that against the world's opposition," people said to convince themselves. Meanwhile the ghetto lived "normally." Some Jews opened shops where one could get anything — even a glass of brandy and some roast meat — for a tidy sum of money. Many people bustled about, doing business with another man's last shirt and jacket.

Some Jews acquired hand-mills, ground a pound of grain and baked themselves some cheap bread. We did not live in complete peace, but "under the devil's broom." The Brown Shirts never allowed us to forget them, and often arrested intellectuals and popular radicals, especially lawyers and religious leaders. The latter took cover under other professions. Those who were arrested never saw freedom again and were murdered.

From time to time "guests" — Gestapo officers — appeared in the ghetto, and with drawn revolvers entered the houses of the wealthier Jews and searched them carefully, stealing money and jewelry and disappearing again.

The Wehrmacht did not sit by with folded arms, either. They took fur, woolen clothing and brass and copper utensils from their victims. Everything was handed over to the *Judenrat*, on pain of death. Hundreds of Jewish slaves in the ghetto manufactured felt boots for the military authorities, as well as wooden things for the army. The *Judenrat* paid millions in contributions, collecting jewelry, quietly giving costly gifts to the hangmen while bowing abjectly to their demands. But that changed nothing. On the contrary, the enemy became even more savage.

The war was at a standstill. Despite furious German attacks, there were no real changes on the Russian front. The goddess of war smiled upon the Soviet Union. Hitler launched another "ingenious" offensive, and cut a narrow path to Stalingrad. The propaganda machine trumpeted the "great victory" in scary fashion. The newspapers were filled with images of Brown Shirts in Stalingrad who rejoiced that they were in control of the Volga. It was curious, though, how Moscow and Leningrad vanished from the German war vocabulary. The average German was supposed to think that the Führer marched beyond those cities and reached Stalingrad.

Military experts quibbled, and said it was a Soviet maneuver to split the German forces. The jokers in the ghetto cracked, "Not bad. Russia's big enough; it can have the pleasure of German cemeteries in Stalingrad."

That's how ghetto Jews laughed at Hitler's strategy.

In early autumn, there were persistent rumors about the Jews of Grodno being sent somewhere to work. As time went on, more and more "reliable" people spoke of it. At the same time, a number of bold Jews escaped from the gruesome Treblinka death camp. The news about the annihilation of the Jews in that camp spread through the larger Jewish settlements like wildfire.

The transports were going to Malkinia, a village approximately eight kilometers from Treblinka, where they were gassed and then cremated.

"Ach!" many Jews argued. "How do I know what they're saying? Just burning people like that! The whole world isn't forsaken yet!"

But the stories of the showers and gas lodged deep in our hearts, left us no rest and robbed us of our sleep. It made itself at home in our heads, demanding to be believed, if only because of its originality. The enemy led them to the showers, gave them soap and towels. This was what the not very bright, cynical murderers were capable of. But once more that constant counselor, reason, came along and, as always at the edge of the abyss, consoled me again, strengthening my hope and making me believe that we would probably survive.

Time, however had other ideas. My thoughts deceived me and my hope led me astray. Summer was soon over, taking with it the sun's last rays and leaving gray skies and windy days in its wake. The trees on the other side of the ghetto fence stood bare, like frayed willow twigs, swaying in the wind and wailing for the vanished days of summer. Mischievous clouds raced across the sky, uncovering a patch of blue here and there and then covered it up again.

I managed to harvest the first fruits of my garden and prepared for a quite comfortable winter. I covered the cottage with clay, and waited for the arrival of "Uncle Snow."

The first day in October brought a surprise. The ghetto was surrounded by a dense cordon of gendarmes. They did not allow workers into the town, and we were completely isolated. People gathered in small groups, talking, talking and talking more, interrupting one another as always, wracking their brains about the sealing-off of the ghetto, and voiced various wild hypotheses, wanting to deceive themselves. They besieged the *Judenrat*, but the officials there knew nothing or chose to remain silent, so that the masses would not rage against them.

In the afternoon, the tension increased. The enemy troops were leading peasants' carts along the ghetto fence. In them were Jews from the provinces — half-naked old men, women and children — huddled against each other. Blue from the cold wind, with small bundles in their hands, they were being taken from Grodno to the infamous Kielbasin camp, where Jewish prisoners of war had been kept, and almost all of them died of typhus. Those people lay in the carts like tethered sheep, their silent glances asking us where they were being taken.

The cordon consisted mostly of civilian Hitlerites, Brown Shirt businessmen and factory owners who came to "dig for gold" in the occupied territories. They went about with drawn pistols, often firing into the air, frightening their victims — who were in any case half-dead — to death. At the head of the procession was a Polish militiaman, dressed for a festival. With his white gloves and well-polished boots, he set the pace, and the mourning procession fell in with its rhythm. The creature marched ahead, beaming and smiling, happy that destiny had granted him — an ordinary Polish peasant — the merit of ridding the Jewish *shtetls* of Jews and being Himmler's comrade.

On October 4, a poster appeared in the ghetto, written in Yiddish and signed by the *Judenrat*. "In accordance with a decision by the German authorities" a large number of the Jews were to be "removed from the ghetto to labor camps in Upper Silesia. All are to take one set of working clothes, one dress suit, a towel, a bowl and spoon, toothbrush, shoe-brush and clothes-brush, and food for three days. The composition of the transports will be announced separately. Head of the *Judenrat*. Zatsay, Advocate."

Some Jews reassured themselves, "What does it mean? We've read it black on white. We're going to Upper Silesia to work." Then they quibbled: "Why would it be worth their while to write that they're sending us to work? If they wanted to kill us, they could do that outside the town, after all."

That is how the optimists, believing the *Judenrat*, argued with the crowd. We suffered through tormented days and sleepless nights. The question "What will happen?" nibbled at our minds. Thick cigars of cheap rolling tobacco helped bear the load of thinking, scheming and searching for a way out. But for the time being, the circle was hermetically sealed and we could not come up with anything.

At night, I sat by a small oil lamp made from a little bottle, and calmed my agitated nerves with books by Sholem Aleichem that I found in an acquaintance's place. Sholem Aleichem's humor affected me like good wine, and by "going for a walk" in Kasrilevke, Mazepevke and Kozodoyevke, I forgot all my troubles. The language of Tevye the milkman and the letters of Sheyne-Sheyndl dispelled my gloom, allowing me to linger in another world.

Sometimes I would burst into hearty laughter in the middle of the night, waking my wife. She completely failed to understand what my joy was about and why I was laughing. My wife began to prepare very seriously for the journey, baking bread, cooking beans until they were dry and sewing rucksacks to hold our few poor possessions.

My six-year-old daughter, on the other hand, was tumbling about carefree, not in the least worried by our troubles.

I once asked my wife, "Are you really serious about going to Hitler's labor camp?"

She raised her sad eyes, and answered me, as usual, with a question: "What? You won't go? Don't you see how all our neighbors are preparing for the journey?"

"Very well," I joked, "Go in good health and write me to tell me how your life is there. Then I'll join you. Until then, I'm not going," I said with determination, "It's better to die where we are."

The senior *Judenrat* officials and officers who liaised with the Gestapo collected gold, diamonds and dollars from the wealthier people who were sent, to the detriment of the qualified workers, to the Ghetto No. 1. The *Judenrat* was besieged by relatives and acquaintances, formerly privileged people, who looked for ways of prolonging their lives while abandoning masses of people.

Then another poster appeared, announcing that anyone caught spreading rumors — that people were going to death instead of to labor camps — would be shot. They also listed the streets that would be the first to be sent to "work." The simple folk rebelled again. Wagon drivers, porters and artisans went to the *Judenrat*, and created a to-do about why their street, of all streets, was to be the first to go.

"Why?" they screamed. "When it comes to distributing potatoes and meat, you always start with the streets where the rich people live!"

But there was no one to scream at. Most of the *Judenrat's* officials vanished into Ghetto No. 1 as that seemed to have a long life expectancy. Embittered people went into the streets, seizing the community leaders who were left by the throat — hitting them, kicking them and pouring out their hearts.

The first deportation was supposed to leave the following morning. Once again I tried to gamble with my life. I took my wife and child to the gate, where many "selected" people stood, waiting for the Gestapo to take them to Ghetto No. 1, according to lists of "needed workers." And while the Gestapo officer hid his face in his hands to light a cigarette, I sneaked into the line of the "fortunate ones" with my little family and was "reincarnated" in the Ghetto No. 1.

CHAPTER 13

Hiding in the Ghetto

In narrow, crooked little streets, between the study-houses and the bathhouse, some 15,000 Jews were crammed together, rubbing up against one another even when going for a walk. Black mud that stank of urine and human excrement lay in streets. Far from any trees, from the horizon or the sunrise, the ghetto seemed like Noah's Ark, or perhaps a big prison cell. As in a beehive, every Jew went about his own business — whether kosher or *treyf* — as long as there was money to be earned to buy bread. The crowded rooms were out of the ordinary as well. People set up dwelling-places in attics and cellars, in study-houses and even in the bathhouse building bunk beds, one above the other.

Children with worried little faces, whose smiles and laughter had disappeared, crawled about in the mud, talking about business just like the grown-ups. They had become intellectually mature. They never indulged in a smile, and felt the mountain weighing on their chests. Then, soon after we left, the Ghetto No. 2 was liquidated.

Bits of news also arrived about the Jews from the provinces in the Kielbasin camp, six kilometers from Grodno. Our bodies quivered when we heard how one Gestapo bandit, a certain Rinzler, tormented his victims, driving young and old to perform "exercises." He shot those who fell, tortured people by depriving them of water, forced hundreds to die of hunger daily and prevented them from performing their natural bodily functions, as well as using other sadistic ways to destroy people.

Then rumors spread about the liquidation of Ghetto No. 1- that the deportations would begin and soon Grodno would be *Judenrein*. Once again we faced the possibility of losing our life raft. Secretly, people were feverishly preparing hiding places with artfully camouflaged entrances. Such extraordinary plans and magic subterranean caves could only be born in the minds of a people condemned to death.

I decided to join a brigade of workers so that I could legally leave the ghetto each day and scout the situation on the other side of the world. I would leave every morning with a brigade of workers for the nearby military hospital. I could hardly wait to be at the ghetto gate with the other workers, waiting impatiently until the ghetto policeman called out, "Military hospital!" Then I would forge a path through the many workers with my elbows and walk out through the barrier, where the Gestapo man raised his stick up high and counted: "Two, eight, sixteen, twenty-four, thirty."

"Thirty," he would shout to another gendarme, who would write in his book: "Thirty Jews departed for the military hospital."

Our work in the hospital was not hard, but it was "interesting." I had the good fortune to be the coffin master and made eternal "wooden clothes" for Hitler's soldiers. I performed my work with pleasure for those unsuccessful world conquerors, feeling satisfaction deep in my heart because of what they were inflicting on us.

Through the hospital's wide, bright corridors, defeated Brown Shirt fighters from the Russian front crawled about minus arms and legs. Others lay in their beds, babbling among themselves. In a separate room lay an officer, his face yellow with jaundice. I busied myself in his room and cautiously sounded him out about his illness. He did not have to be asked and told me that he received his "blessing" in Leningrad.

"I'm surprised," I said to him naively. "The Germans have such good airplanes, tanks and soldiers and the war isn't over yet."

He looked at the ceiling and said: "We were mistaken. The Russians are much stronger than we thought and their war machine is no worse than ours. Their bombs and tanks are no playthings," he said seriously and with regret. And I shook my head foolishly and stammered: "Aha, aha, now I understand."

People discussed secrets again, while the *Judenrat* was drawing up precise lists of those who would have to go to "work" first. "Hammer, scissors and iron" were first in the firing line. Non-Jewish electricians appeared in the ghetto and installed big lamps, so that at night the ghetto's dark, narrow streets were bright and filled with light, light that entered every hole, preventing people from hiding from death.

The ghetto police went from house to house in precise accordance with the lists, gathering the victims in the Great Synagogue. People went there, resigned, laden with rucksacks and baskets, holding their children by the hand or carrying them in their arms. Thousands of people were crammed into the narrow space, standing on their feet for hours on end, in their own urine, unable to move a limb, lifting their eyes to the ceiling and begging the Creator to have mercy and redeem them.

The "redeemers" arrived early next morning in the form of Ukrainians and gendarmes who, on their last march to the station, chased the masses along with wooden clubs. The police tried to seize me and my little family for deportation. The evening was restless. Station workers returned to the ghetto, and told us that 40 empty railway wagons stood ready on the siding. The workers who did night work were not allowed out of the ghetto. The electric lamps were lit and, as usual, death was in the air.

Then, of all places, my brother, Shlomo Reizer found a hiding-place in the synagogue attic. One floor below it was the hospital where he worked as a medical practitioner. We barely managed to climb the stairs in the darkness and hide in the Byzantine style eaves, when a machine gun chattered, putting the fear of death into the living.

The Angel of Death enjoyed himself in the ghetto, and everyone felt his eerie breath. He filled all the little streets, the cellars and attics. The police were extraordinarily active, searching everywhere with electric lamps and tapping the walls with hammers to see if they were hollow. The Gestapo warned them that if a sufficient number of victims were not assembled by morning, they themselves would be packed up with their wives, brides and children.

People paid great sums of gold for an hour of life — especially when the Gestapo told the police that no harm would come to them, that they would let them live. The policemen worked like angels of destruction to save their own lives. They discovered one hideout after another, from which the stench of nitrogen poured forth. They discovered people with weak nerves who could not stand it, who went mad, dancing, jumping, clapping their hands and singing. (The police took those people to a place where the Gestapo finished them off at a stroke).

Lying in our hiding-place, we heard heavy trucks moving outside the synagogue. They loaded the old, the sick and the children, so that on a frosty night they would not have to struggle to get to the station, some two kilometers distant. They were not particularly careful with the children. The Germans grabbed a little hand or foot or head of young ones from the orphanage and home for foundlings who could not dress themselves, and hurled them into the vehicle. The children's little cries cut through the seven heavens, filling our hiding-place with their wailing.

Early next morning, the nurse (my brother's wife) Peli (Gutman) Reizer came to our hiding-place, pale and shattered, and fell to the floor crying and moaning. She told us she was on duty for the deportation that night and witnessed everything. She beat her head with her fists and complained to God, asking why her heart had not burst. Wailing, she told us: "They took doctors in white aprons, with their instruments, to take part in the mocking game, as if they were "accompanying" the transport. One of them walked a bit drunkenly. He injected himself with poison." She recognized Doctor Klinger, a renowned scholar and venereal specialist from Lodz, who was driven to Grodno in 1939 by the war. He shakily walked his final road.

The following morning they "sniffed out" our hiding-place and we had to disappear. Our instinct for self-preservation allowed us no rest and we skulked about like animals, looking for a hiding-place. On the second day of the "action" we came across one by chance. It was in the very dark cellar of the same synagogue, where there was a big supply of potatoes for the ghetto kitchen. There was a well-camouflaged little brick door 30 centimeters square in a brick enclosure, and it moved on iron hinges. *Judenrat* officials had prepared it for themselves. Through this small hole, which was right near the ground, we crept single file into a small room equipped with electricity, small camp beds, blankets and a corner full of carrots, beets and dry bread. The only thing missing was water.

The Gestapo and the police were still rampaging in the streets and deported about 6,000 people. There were 15 of us in the secret cave, including three doctors, a mother with her daughter, son-in-law and grandchild. The child was barely a year old and cried constantly, exposing us to discovery. His mother gave him something to make him sleep, but barely managed to calm him down.

Minutes stretched out like snakes and hours seemed like years. Above our heads was the concrete floor of the synagogue, where the feet of the assembled Jews drummed continually. Their stamping was accompanied by automatic gunfire, the barking of dogs and strident curses of the gendarmes.

I was near the little door of the cave, and pricked my ears like an animal, trying to hear every rustle on the other side of the wall. The tension exhausted me and my brother replaced me. Then we heard human footsteps on the other side, and the rays of a flashlight penetrated the narrow cracks between the bricks into the darkness of our cave.

We heard German: *"Ist hier niemand da?"* ("Is anyone here?") Our blood froze. A second voice answered: *"Hier ist der Kartoffelkeller des Judenrats."* ("Here is the *Judenrat's* potato cellar").

The steps receded and it became quiet. We understood we were safe for the moment, but could not recover from shock. Our hearts pounded like an axe hits a tree. We couldn't leave. Bursts of machine gun fire were heard and people still moved above us. We hid in that cave for nearly three days and nights. We hardly spoke to each other. We were each engrossed in our own "little worlds," summing up past years of joy and freedom and longingly recalling even the "not so good" years, before this disaster.

Every word was pronounced softly, as at a sick person's bedside, in the knowledge that we were guarding precious life. Our fear, excitement and nervousness induced a kind of sleepiness, which we fought so that we would not snore. I did not enjoy waking the doctor every few minutes. She was more than 60 years old and snored loudly.

We had a little tin box with honey and enough bread to eat, which we prepared earlier in case we needed to find a place to hide. While I prepared I prayed, "Please God, make it so we'll never need this!"

The sweet honey made us very thirsty, but there was not a drop of water to quench it. Basheleh was moaning, tossing about, demanding something to drink. But she understood the danger and did not make loud noises. Leaving our hideout to find water was out of the question.

I dug a nail out of my pocket, and pierced a few holes in the tin cover of the honey container, crushed a few beets on it and quenched my child's thirst with the juice. Soon after that, the street became quieter. The shooting stopped and the movement of people above our heads abated. The doctor was wearing a watch and we knew it was 10 o'clock in the morning.

We couldn't think of what to do next. We were afraid the Gestapo and the gendarmes had taken everyone from the ghetto and that only we remained. What would our lives be like then? What would we do? We were also not sure if the *aktion* had subsided completely. Maybe this was a police trick to lull those still in hiding out into the street? We brooded, but didn't come to a conclusion.

"I'll crawl out and sniff around a bit," I called out softly. I took off my shoes so that no one would hear them squeak, and was ready to crawl out. My little daughter took hold of my legs, nestled against me with her whole body trembling and begged me, "Daddy, don't go away, don't go away!"

She was prepared to make a racket and would not let go. I had to abandon my plan and then a terrified silence reigned. The doctor's wrist watch ticked, cutting the hours and seconds into tiny fragments. Now and then someone tossed and turned to get some relief from the little pebbles and pieces of brick on the floor that jabbed at us through our clothes. (We put the few small beds with blankets at the disposal of mothers with small children).

Then we heard sure footsteps the other side of the little door. The wooden box camouflaging the entrance to our cave creaked. Someone tried to push the door open and our blood froze. We doubled up, became smaller and our hearts slowed.

I decided, "I'm not going anywhere. Let this be my grave!" Someone stubbornly continued to push at the little door and called out, "Open up! Don't be afraid, we're Jews!"

"Jews! They're Jews," we whispered joyfully to one another, feeling instinctively that they were actually Jews. I opened the little door, switched on the electricity, and an elderly Jewish man poked his head in and announced: "Go, brothers, you're free! It's all over now."

Every one of us was ready to fall into the arms of this redeeming angel and to kiss him for the joyful news.

CHAPTER 14

Mourning the Dead

First we asked for water and they brought a bucketful. We quenched our thirst, and emptied the bucket in no time. The Jews wondered how we found their hideout.

"Your hideout is worth much gold, brother," I replied and thanked him.

In the three previous days, 10,000 Jews were deported from the ghetto. Many were shot dead in the streets and in their houses. Some 4,000 Jews remained — the most essential workers. They told us that people were hoping that the deportations were over.

We carefully crawled out, and camouflaged the space well in case we needed it again. I thought, "May God grant, we'll never need this."

We walked into the street and once more saw the bright light of the sun. The fresh air entered our stale lungs, allowing us to breathe deeply. The daylight dazzled us, so we squinted to bear it.

A wet, sticky snow fell thinly on the ground, covering the black, muddy pavement. It was unable to cover puddles of blood that seeped out from beneath, crying out to Heaven. Ghetto Jews hastily gathered up the dead and took them to the nearly 300 year-old cemetery inside the ghetto. Somewhere near a fence, a dead man lay forgotten. He was on his side, like a swimmer, face pale and stiff, his eyes open and his temples bloody. The wet snow did not cover his face, with fear of death in its expression.

A young boy was shot on a flight of stairs. He wore a navy blue student's coat with gleaming buttons and lay on his back in a puddle of frozen blood that trailed crookedly down the steps. He had a sharp white nose, white child's teeth, and his half-open eyes stared fixedly at the gables above. His father bent over him, babbling something, grimacing as if about to cry, though his eyes were dry. His mother moved around him like a wounded animal, wringing her hands and wailing that her child had "not been careful" and so met a violent death.

In the narrow little streets there were scattered heaps of ragged pillows, featherbeds and blankets. The doors to many apartments stood open, strangely inviting us in and then chasing out, scaring us with emptiness that told of vanished householders. A fire flickered gloomily in a tiled stove. Above the burned wood, its blue tongues licked the stove's door, demanding something to consume. There was a wooden trough with leavened dough in the corner. Apparently someone tried to bake a loaf of bread, but had no time to finish. The dough, left rising for too long, hissed and groaned as if asking why it hadn't been put in the oven.

The beds were stripped, pillows ripped open. Underwear, bedspreads, clothes, dishes, porcelain dolls and cheap jewelry were thrown around in open drawers and were crushed underfoot. An old-fashioned wall clock ticked monotonously. Beneath its pendulum there hung a picture of a naked child playing.

The torn picture album on the table told of three generations; there were grandmothers in wigs; grandfathers in skullcaps, with big religious books and bony fingers. They sat on gleaming, polished chairs, their parchment faces gazing out indifferently; young people, who looked familiar, smiled, "caught" on their walks, arm-in-arm on park benches, or happy on the beach at the Nieman River; laughing little children; quiet, well-poised children with bicycles and schoolbooks; classes with their teachers on Chanukah or in Purim plays in full regalia. The photographs cried clamorously from the album's pages: "But we were just here!" They seemed to eerily ask, "Why us and not you?"

The heavy snow stopped and was beginning to melt. The old cemetery gate was wide open, "inviting" curious passers-by to look. Inside, people were laid out in orderly rows like bundles of colored rags, with true German precision. Nearer the gate a few dozen corpses looked as if they had just been thrown there. There were mangled heads and skull-bones hanging from pieces of hairy head-flesh. They had been shot with dum-dum bullets and were unrecognizable.

The living looked for relatives among the dead, trying to identify remains through their clothing. They conjectured about the identity of the corpses according to a padded coat, a pair of trousers or shoes. Deeper inside the burial grounds were the corpses that were shot conventionally. The crows picked out their eyes and tore white pieces of flesh from around the sockets. The eyeless victims lay on their backs, gazing at the gray sky from their big eye sockets. When I saw the first victim, I wanted to vomit and was shaken, but the human eye gets used to things, and feelings probably get hardened as well.

A young couple in their early 20s died holding hands. They were decently dressed, and you couldn't see where the bullets did their work. She wore new women's snow boots and silk stockings, her round shiny legs protruded from her short black coat. She lay nestled against her husband's side, as if resting after a walk. Her face was a lively pink, her black eyes open under fine women's eyebrows and looked as if she were counting the clouds. Her husband's face was chalk white, his eyes slits, his cheeks hollow, emphasizing his cheekbones and jaw. His dark autumn suit, yellow shoes and winter coat without a yellow star probably meant that they'd been caught in town with false papers and that Polish police had handed them over to Kurt Wiese, Nazi commandant of the ghetto.

Beyond them lay the suicides — those who took poison. They did not want to roam far from their parents' bones and home towns, so they ended the torture with potassium cyanide or Luminal. They were mostly intellectuals, some elderly doctors. A dentist wore his best suit, creased patent leather shoes and an old-fashioned white shirt-front with a black bow tie. His yellow face was turned to the sky, eyes like slits and teeth clenched.

Gershune, the midwife, was a lonely woman with no family. There she lay, poisoned, the lower half of her body sewn into a sheet up to her armpits. Pinned to this home-sewn, unfinished shroud was a little note, written in Yiddish in blue ink, "I ask to be buried according to Jewish law."

Then there were the rows of the dead, laid out like wooden beams in a saw mill. Women, men and children, young and old, lay waiting for someone to hack open the frozen soil and bury them for their eternal rest — a redeemed people, all sorrows gone.

The surviving Jews, who were "racially impure," were still the best and most necessary workers, so the Gestapo allowed them to live for the moment. They bustled about the ghetto confusedly and didn't recognize each other.

They carried beds, cupboards and all their goods and chattel to the two remaining legal streets assigned to them after the deportation. They were separated by a fence from what was once Ghetto No. 1.

Parents mourned for children who were snatched away, and children mourned their vanished parents.

Leibl Reizer, my sister's husband (who was also my cousin) was dragged off. He was an active member of the illegal organization, Poalei Zion, and a well-known philanthropist in the ghetto who established an organization that supported hungry women and children from Eastern Russia. The unfortunates had been left on their own in the ghetto when their husbands were arrested or fled. The abandoned ones had no time to evacuate because of the Germans' lightning attacks.

My sister bemoaned the loss of her husband, and still weeping, told her children to remember the date so they could mark his *yahrtzeit*. I consoled her with brutal words: I told her to stop crying because we weren't safe either and would sooner or later drown in the same stormy waves as the rest of the Jews. Life lost its sparkle. It seemed the struggle to live was utterly in vain, that we would be unable to avoid the fate of the others.

The Kielbasin camp, six kilometers from Grodno, was where the SS bandit Karl Rinzler "liquidated" 24,000 Jews from the provinces. From there they were sent to the ovens of Treblinka and Auschwitz, while some of them were murdered on the spot.

For reasons unknown to this day, the Gestapo sent the last few hundred Jews to our ghetto. They wandered around like living skeletons, hungry and half-naked. Wherever there was a rubbish bin, they fell upon it, searching for food. The regular ghetto Jews, hungry as they were, shared their last morsels of bread with their brothers, and offered them the "edge" of their own beds to sleep on. Some of the former exhausted and despondent inmates from Kielbasin volunteered for deportation. The stronger ones, the stubborn ones, struggled on and later fled to the partisans.

Every day, 4,000 Jews lined up to leave the ghetto for work. I was among them, marching with a dozen skilled workers to the military hospital, near the ghetto fence. All day long, from the other side of the wall, we could hear shots ring out from Wiese's automatic.

Following the deportation, Wiese trained his eye and improved his marksmanship by using Jews for target practice. In most cases, he created excuses. One victim's Star of David was too small, another's too big. This one looked suspicious, that one was impudent. But there were also cases when Wiese shot people for no reason. Those killings took place in the early mornings when Wiese, a mountain infantryman, was overcome by a longing to go hunting.

At such times, he would sneak into the ghetto, hide in the empty buildings and fire at the first victim within a 40–50 meter-range. He aimed right between the eyes of his victims, who would soundlessly collapse. If he failed to hit them, Wiese would seethe with rage, spit and curse — *"Sakrament, Donnerwetter"* and shoot the next Jew right between the eyes.

The Jews avoided Wiese like a conflagration. If they noticed him, even from afar, they quickly vanished and the streets were deserted.

Yeshaye Kaganovitsh, my carpentry boss at the hospital, pushed us to work fast. Hitler's men liked feudal, aristocratic looking furniture. They often demanded that the Jewish workers furnish their rooms, and promised the master craftsman to intercede on our behalf if there were a deportation. Our boss took this at face value and rushed our work all the more. I would often cool him down, saying: "Yeshaye, don't hurry so, don't rush our work so. We can't avoid the showers forever."

At such moments, he would put his plane down, remain standing frozen for a while, look out the window into the hospital courtyard and say, as if talking to himself, "Is it really true what people say? That they're suffocating people with gas and burning them in an oven?"

CHAPTER 15

New Year's Eve 1943

One frosty morning, the door of the workshop was hastily opened and the hospital's supply officer entered in a cloud of icy mist. He ordered me to make two coffins and bring them to the morgue.

I applied myself diligently to this "good deed" and they soon were finished. When I brought them to the morgue, there were two dead men on the floor — German soldiers, frightfully maimed, their hands and feet torn off. They were dressed like infantrymen and one of them wore a sleeve that bore the inscription '*Zugführer*' (platoon leader).

"From a railway disaster!" the officer said ambiguously to a soldier standing at his side.

I diligently nailed the coffins shut and decoded "railway disaster" to mean a military train on its way to the Russian front that was blown up by partisans. I went cheerfully back to the workshop and told my friends what the partisans had done. We drank to each other's health with small doses of furniture polish and hoped we would soon have more such good news to celebrate. But I was impatient to get back to the ghetto to see whether Frumke and Basheleh were still alive, and feverishly thought about ways for us to escape.

Not long after that, the officer from the morgue came to the joiner's workshop, ordered me to bring my tools and asked me to build shelves in the hospital's clothing depot. There, he unlocked a cabinet stocked with revolvers, took each one in his hands, tried the safety locks, put in magazines and wrote their numbers down in a little notebook. I sneaked a peek at the gleaming revolvers and had an idea. My heart beat violently and I almost lost it. But I got myself under control and cheerfully knocked the boards for the shelves together with my hammer. I now knew that the cabinet contained the miracle I was looking for. Escape was now possible.

The officer left me to my work, and when I knew he was gone, I examined the cabinet's locks and hinges. I also checked the windows, inside and out, to see how they were built. I was certain this secret was going to come in handy, and did not breathe a word about it to anyone.

The partisans were very popular. They evoked the fear of death in the Brown Shirts. The peasants who came to the ghetto said that they themselves had seen partisans and that they came to the peasants mainly at night to get food. But these were rumors, and no one knew how to contact them.

By sheer coincidence, and in secret, I discovered that one of my friends had been to "those places" and knew someone. He was a young butcher who knew the region like the back of his hand, and one day, he and a friend, taking a risk, disguised themselves as non-Jews to take a walk in the forests and villages to meet "them" face to face.

At first, my young man was reticent, but I got under his skin. He finally opened up, and told me that about 100 kilometers from the town, in a small White Russian village hidden in the dense Nacza Forest, he spoke with "the man himself" — Kostia Bucko, organizer of a group of Russian and Jewish partisans. Bucko asked him to recruit people from the ghetto, but they had to come with weapons.

"The main thing is guns," he said. "Our group is big enough."

"I'll get you the guns," I said to his astonishment, and asked him to get me to Bucko. To my delight, the group's technical organizer was Chanan Elgin, a friend. In a small house, by the dim light of an oil lamp, behind a blacked out window, we made plans to get the weapons to the group. In exchange, my family and I would join them and come under their protection. They agreed to the deal, but we had to carry them out that very night.

At that point, 24 people were ready to join the partisans and would travel in two big sleighs with coachmen and strong horses, so we had to move fast. I needed two bold, young accomplices, and soon two teenagers, barely 18, came into our dark little room, looked at me with respect and sat down at the table. The cruel times had made them reckless and bold. They faced life with youthful exuberance and natural courage. They'd been pulled off the transports and were considered very good partisans.

The one sitting nearest me was skinny, and with a confident look, gave me his hand and introduced himself as Beryl. He was smoking an English pipe to banish the strong smell of moonshine that emanated from him. "You're drunk," I said reproachfully, "You won't understand what I'm saying."

"Speak, speak. We'll understand everything," said the other one. He went by the name of Pinye and was short, with a white face and Jewish nose. "A bit of schnapps gives courage," he said, rolling a cigarette in a piece of newspaper.

"All right, then. But remember that we'll be doing a serious bit of work that reeks of death and we need to have our wits about us."

I drew a map of the hospital on a piece of paper, showed them where the window was and where the cupboard with the guns stood. I went through everything with them. They looked at the piece of paper with boyish curiosity and finally said: "Why do we need plans? Come and show us the place and we'll get it over and done with."

I agreed, and told them to prepare a small pair of pliers and a chisel. I went off to tell Frumke to get ready for the journey. I couldn't tell her everything because she might oppose my crazy plan — which I believed had more chance of failing than succeeding. I told her to dress warmly, to bring Basheleh and prepare something to eat in a little basket. She was to meet me at the barbed wire. Frumke realized I was dead serious and didn't ask for whys and wherefores.

The people who shared our room noticed our whispering and constantly asked me to let them in on our secret. Were we withholding information about an imminent deportation? An elderly woman cried and asked me to have mercy on her and tell her everything I was telling my wife. I swore several different ways that what we were talking about had nothing to do with deportations and was a private family matter.

I went to see my sister and brother and their families in the room they shared. I busied myself in a corner and looked at the dear, lovely children, who were so close to my heart. To my great distress, there was no way I could help them and had no idea if the plans we made would work. In my heart and soul I said good-bye to them. My devoted sister saw me changing my shoes late in the evening and noticed my absent-mindedness. She guessed something was up, gave me a pair of woolen socks, told me to put them on and did not speak again.

Outside, in the dark, I kissed my wife, told her to get ready and quickly left to join my new companions. Since the deportations, the ghetto was strictly guarded. Gendarmes with automatic weapons walked around on the other side of the barbed wire, as if it was a prison full of dangerous criminals, and cast constant glances at the ghetto fence, which lay high up on the hill. In the distance one could see the frozen Nieman River and fishermen's houses enveloped in snow. Their bright little windows signaled to us, calling to us to come into the happy world.

In the light of an electric street lamp, a gendarme walked about slowly, step by step, his hobnail boots striking the frozen pavement, as he cast frequent glances toward the ghetto. We observed the patrol route for quite some time, then tore the Stars of David off our clothes. When the gendarme had his back turned, we ran quickly down the hill and appeared almost under his very nose, whistling and uttering un-Jewish curses. The gendarme must have wondered at the impertinence of the Polish boys making such a racket so late in the evening. Our feet moved easily, as if dancing. A feeling of confidence seized our hearts and encouraged us.

We soon stood at the hospital fence, snipping the fence's braided wires with a small pair of pliers. Each wire snapped with a whistling sound, enlarging the hole we had to pass through. The civilian and German pedestrians took no particular notice of the "hospital workers" who stayed so late to repair the fence. My young co-workers had indulged in a little schnapps and probably did not appreciate the seriousness of the moment. On the other hand, for me, those few minutes seemed terribly long and I began to tremble. Beryl noticed and "encouraged" me with a Russian curse.

In almost no time, we stood at the window of the clothing depot and opened the summer casement windows. Opening the winter windows was more difficult — we had to remove the putty from the window pane, but we shattered it, and the sound of breaking glass treacherously resounded in the night-time silence.

Quick as devils, Beryl and Pinye were in the room. The sound of creaking wood told my carpenter's ear that they were at the cabinet. In the semi-darkness of the hospital courtyard, electric torches were lit. Germans talked among themselves. Soldiers laughed throatily in a hospital room. Nearby, the steps of the guard could be heard as he vigilantly watched over the patients in the enemy zone. My companions passed a heavy cigar box through the window and jumped out.

In a nearby narrow little street, we examined our trophies: two pistols (one source says they had four pistols), one Parabellum and almost 200 bullets with magazines. "Wasn't there more?" I asked my companions angrily. But the boys were fussing over the "shooters," literally kissing them, and did not reply.

One of them went to give the sign that all was well and I went to the meeting place. Soon the rest of our group arrived, including my wife and daughter, who stood hidden in the shadows of the narrow little street. There were 13 of us. Another 13 were supposed to wait for us on the eastern side highway, outside the city limits.

We walked quickly and fanned out. It was a two kilometer walk, but we had to get across town and took numerous detours to avoid the police. I took my daughter in my arms, gave her strict instructions not to talk, buried my typically Jewish nose in her little clothes, and with rapid steps followed my friends, who ran as if they were being chased.

It was almost dark and very cold. People passed us by, wrapped in their own coats. It probably never occurred to them to check us out, though we were walking fast. A flashlight flared up a few times behind us, its light touching our shoulders lightly, before it finally disappeared down another street. We cut across the railroad tracks at the train station. There were brightly lit carriages with soldiers in them, waiting to pull out. We took a little side street at the very edge of town, and almost ran the rest of the way to the fields where the sleighs were waiting.

It was difficult to carry Basheleh such a long distance and maintain my speed. I panted heavily and called out to my companions: "Comrades, don't run so fast!" But it was no use. They ran as if dogs were at their heels and pretended not to hear me.

The second group, hidden for several days in a small village with the horses and sleighs, arrived punctually at the agreed upon spot. We briefly squeezed each other's hands before we climbed in and set off on our journey. It was late on the night of February 7, 1943. The air was frozen and the sky was full of stars. The snow squeaked beneath the weight of the fully-loaded sleigh. The horses lifted their feet joyfully and, at a gallop, carried us away from the ghetto.

After we covered three kilometers, we stopped at a pit that was once used as a horse cemetery. My companions leapt joyfully from the sleighs, climbed into the trench and started loading their guns. Unfortunately, the bullets were too large, but we were able to match a few magazines to the Parabellum. At that moment, someone in the group suggested we choose a commander whose orders we would follow, and to my surprise, he suggested me.

In the semi-darkness I looked at the faces of my comrades, mostly simple folk, "men of the people". Some of them had grown up in a *petit bourgeois*, undisciplined environment. They were stiff-necked people, who would find it difficult to be subjected to discipline. But as I assessed the seriousness of the moment, and my honest comrades' glances, I agreed to accept the position and said, "Comrades, we'll be taking uncharted paths to look for the partisans. The journey is dangerous, so I accept your suggestion on one condition — that you do everything I ask. I hope I won't lead you astray."

"Agreed, agreed!" they all roared in unison. One of them even called out: "Shoot anyone who disobeys!"

My first order was to get quickly back into the sleighs. We followed a trail in the fields to avoid dangerous encounters on the highway. But after we covered 10 kilometers, we had to move back to the highway because the trail was impassable.

My companions were joyful and animated. We inhaled, filling our chests with the fresh, cold air. The frost pinched our cheeks and froze our fingers. A gentle little wind whistled continuously, whispering: "It's good. It's good."

The horses ran faster on the smooth and empty highway and our eyes pierced the darkness to make sure that no one approached us. My little daughter lay snuggled close to her mother, drunk with fresh air, sleeping soundly.

Someone hauled a big bottle of moonshine out from beneath the straw on the sleigh and offered everyone a little drink. I protested and said it was not time to get drunk. But he replied quite cold-bloodedly, "Whoever doesn't drink booze, will drink tar."

It was the same fellow who earlier suggested that I shoot those who disobey. I kept quiet and decided in my heart, "Let whatever happens happen, but I won't give any more orders to people who hate discipline." The further away from Grodno we got, the less dangerous it became, though peril still loomed. We had to cross the border from the Third Reich into White Russia, 50 kilometers away, that very night, and get far away from it by morning. Our coachmen whipped the horses unsparingly and they caught up the kilometers.

Chanan Elgin, the group's organizer, sneaked his 60-year-old mother out of the ghetto, and she sat in our sleigh. Avreymel, Shloime and Velvel Pave, brothers who owned one sleigh, reproached Elgin for dragging his elderly mother along when younger people were being deported. The old woman sat quietly and said nothing. I made them understand that old people wanted to live just as much as young ones. The three Pave brothers were simple, kindhearted folk, wagon drivers who later distinguished themselves as partisans and sacrificed their young lives on the altar of freedom. But at that moment, they could simply not understand why an old woman would want to live.

From a distance, the sides of the highway appeared solid black. Every eight to 10 kilometers there was a small village and here and there a dim light burned in a small window. After almost three hours' ride, we were near Skidel, 32 kilometers from Grodno. To the left of the highway, we could see the dark outlines of the *shtetl* through which I had fled to Minsk almost two years earlier.

We whipped the horses rigorously to make them fly through the area so that we wouldn't encounter any "demons" on the highway. As we journeyed on, a sleigh filled with peasants moved toward us. They were delivering grain to the occupied warehouses in Grodno and stared at us goggle-eyed and surprised. We brought our heads close together, one against the other, to make ourselves look like large bundles in the darkness. The peasants thought we looked suspicious and egged their horses on, probably sensing that we carried no ordinary merchandise.

With every passing kilometer, the load of worries on our backs, which every living Jew carried in the ghetto, became smaller and the weight on our souls lighter — we were finally in a world without barbed wire. The snow-covered bushes and woods along the highway aroused hope in our hearts. Among them we might find protection.

It was past midnight, when, a few kilometers from the border, we heard the bells of a small hunting sleigh in the distance, and they became louder. Soon we could see the outlines of two white horses running in the opposite direction. We were a little confused until the small sleigh passed us. It was carrying two gendarmes with automatic weapons, probably border guards. One of them shouted in bad Russian: *"Kuda vi yedete?"* (Where are you going?)

The second fully-laden sleigh was right behind us. The Germans were probably afraid of that many people near the border so late at night, and hastily whipped up their horses and disappeared. Of course, we did the same.

We turned our sleighs into the fields, toward the border. The sleighs sank into deep snow that almost reached the horses' bellies. Our faithful horses sweated and panted, their flanks heaving as they led us swiftly along. The border area was bare, with no bushes at all. Our dark clothes and the brown horses against the white snow could betray us, even from afar.

We could see the large brick customs house in the distance, brightly lit, and we wanted to get around it as quickly as possible. We got off the sleighs to make it easier for the horses, and held fast to the sides so as not to fall behind. It was difficult and almost beyond our strength to struggle in the drifts of snow, which came to our waists. Hot sweat covered our faces and glued our shirts to our bodies. Our companions were panting in short and heavy gasps as we furtively crossed the border between death and life. Two of our team went ahead and poked at the barbed wire that fenced off White Russia from the Third Reich.

Then Shepsl and Peyshke announced that we were in White Russia.

We entered a dense little wood and flung ourselves into the snow, pleased to get some rest and give our horses something to chew on. Peyshke Manes was the owner and driver of the second sleigh. He was a healthy-looking, strong fellow with a pair of wagon driver's arms. Like the Pave brothers, he was a simple, good-hearted man with an amazing sense of direction. Only later did it become apparent what a precious gift he had. His sense of direction was like a compass, and he never led us astray on the roads and in the forest.

There were 26 of us from Grodno on those sleighs: Peyshke, his wife Chaike and their 4 year-old daughter Dinele; his brother Leibl, also a coachman; his sister Sonia Epstein, (who had been an employee at Shapiro's Wines), her husband Kadish Epstein (son of Epstein, the civil servant at the municipal authorities); the three brothers Pave, Avreymel, Shloime and Velvl, who owned one of the sleighs; Chanan Elgin, a carpenter and his mother, Tzivia, a former worker in Shereshevski's factory.

There were Avrom Kapulski, a butcher from Fershtot (suburb of Grodno) and his young son Hirshele. The father was a butcher who liked a drop of booze and was a respectable fighter against the Germans. His young son, a 14-year-old pipsqueak, later stirred up the entire region and received the highest commendations for his daring heroism and the large number of Germans he notched onto his belt.

Shepsel Garbulski — also a butcher (grandson of Hirsh the Butcher); Beryl Lipski — a transport worker from Fershtot was a healthy-looking, sturdy fellow, a transport worker, strong and agile, whose fists inspired fear in a remarkable number of young people. He later became a heroic partisan and the detachment fussed over him proudly. He was with his cousin, my young accomplice in the gun theft was Beryl Lipski — a shoemaker.

There was Pinchas Mazavyetski, a young lad (son of the chicken dealer Solday from Yurzik, Yedidye Kaminski — a butcher from Fershtot; Leizer Sisun (nicknamed "Tratra"), also a butcher; Zeidel Ash — a young lad; Chaya-Leah Berlin — a girl from Skidel; Yankel Levin, a young boy from Fershtot; Moishe Kayles, son-in-law of the butcher Avreymel "Bants"; and then there were the three of us, Frumke, née Gordon, Bashele and me.

Moishe Kayles, Zeidke Ash, Leizer Sisun, Yankel Levin, and Chanan Elgin picked up partisans' rifles to take bloody revenge for their murdered kin. Some of them sacrificed their lives in battle. Kadik and Sonia Epstein and Peyshke Manes once spent time in the woods we were in. They'd been there for 10 days during a terrible frost, unable to contact anyone and bitterly returned to the ghetto. Sonia suffered frostbitten toes and developed gangrene. We talked quietly and smoked masses of cheap rolling tobacco while making plans to find a place to stay during the day.

Little by little the sky lightened and the stars were slowly extinguished. The crowing of cocks could be heard in the distance and it was time to hide. We continued for a few more kilometers and went into a dense stand of pine trees. By the time we gathered twigs to make a fire for warmth, it was already bright. We were all worried about leaving sleigh tracks in the snow that could lead the wrong people to our site. We posted guards with guns at the edge of the woods. We ate with gusto, drank some brandy and felt great because we had escaped the grave.

The guards sent us a signal around noon. Near the campsite, a Polish man, pale and nervous, told us that he was the forester. He noticed the tracks in the snow and came to see what was going on. For safety's sake, we took his passport, copied down his name and house number and warned him that if he informed the gendarmerie, we would settle the score. He crossed himself, looked in terror at our guns and assured us he would keep quiet.

We rejoiced as night fell and it began to snow lightly, so that it was safe to continue our journey. Our surroundings seemed impenetrable. The horses, rested and fed, covered the kilometers with pleasure, and carried us closer to our goal. Our companions sat in the sleighs, continually humming a song from the Bialystok Ghetto:

> In the Bialystok Ghetto every heart aches.
> We're sitting and thinking:
> What fate will we meet?
> With the star on our lapels,
> They chase us and beat us in the street…

We wanted to live. Joyful thoughts chased away the melancholy mood and we sensed that good things were coming.

CHAPTER 16

Fleeing

This material is taken from the conclusion of In the Struggle and a subsequent series of articles that were combined to remove redundancies, and to maintain the chronology and style of this book, Ed.

We were careful and tried to avoid garrisons. Sometimes we added kilometers to the trip when we detoured to a safer route. In some places, the trail was snowed in and at the intersections we groped around with our fingers to feel for the main road, and judging it by the depths of the ruts. We lit matches in the dark and argued about which road to take. Peyshke had the "veto," laid down routes, and indicated the direction with a wave of his hand — left or right — and said confidently: "Go this way." He was always right and we always got to where we wanted to be.

We avoided asking peasants for directions, since some of them were cunning and would lead the gendarmes to us in a heartbeat. Many Polish peasants, in exchange for a few kilograms of salt, lent a hand to the annihilation of the Jews in the provinces and helped the gendarmerie set up ambushes to capture escaping Jews. (This was a popular Gestapo tactic in White Russia).

Sometimes, in the evenings, when we had no choice and had to ask a peasant for directions, we would confuse him by asking him about all the roads in the area. We wanted to know where all of them went, and would not say which route we chose. Once the peasant gave us information, we would decide how to get where we needed to go. But the peasant didn't know where we were really headed or how we were getting there.

We'd gone 80 kilometers and were near the small town of Wasiliski. It was growing light and we could make out the church steeple on the horizon. We detoured because the town housed a large police garrison that specialized in capturing Jews trying to hide in the Nacza woods.

Soon the church disappeared and we were in an open snow-covered area with no sign of forest or bushes. It was a bright morning, and we were as visible as the "palm of a hand" in the white fields. We had to disappear, fast. There was a farmhouse in the distance and we urged our horses in that direction. We had no choice but to seek a hiding-place with an unknown peasant.

A peasant woman was alone in the cottage. She shook with fear, asked no questions and agreed to everything we asked. She told us to take the sleighs into the large barns used for storing grain and suggested we crawl into the depths of the haystacks in the stable. The homely warmth of the peasant's cottage enveloped us deliciously, warming our frozen limbs. The smell of fresh-baked bread and freedom and kept us there, as if by force, just so we could enjoy it a bit more.

The peasant woman cooked something warm, and we ate with hearty appetites. We posted guards and crept into the deep, fragrant hay in the barn. We'd been in the cold for almost three days and nights, so it was hard to get warm. The final images from the ghetto haunted our minds. But our extreme fatigue overcame us and brought true, healthy sleep.

We woke in the afternoon, and it was already dark. Stars appeared as we hurried to continue our journey. By that time, the peasant's husband had returned from Lida, and was at first frightened when he saw us. When we explained we weren't thieves and would not take anything from him, he calmed down, gave us some home-grown tobacco and advised us to go to a forest 40 kilometers' away, where 5,000 people were in hiding.

We told him, smiling, that we were headed in the opposite direction, but took his information as the truth. We did indeed follow his directions in the darkness. The further we went, the closer we came to the forests, human inhabitants were rarely to be seen.

Along the way, we stopped at rich peasants' homes, shook awake the sleepy owners, and sent in a delegation to demand food. The peasants did not refuse us — out of respect for our guns — and gave us bread, pig's fat and other foodstuffs. In one place, my companions were given a calf, which they slaughtered in the snow and stowed on the sleigh. One peasant gave us a bucket of tallow. We "borrowed" a saw and an axe from one peasant, so that we would be able to build a cabin in the forest.

By daybreak we were in a dense forest. Giant pine trees and fir trees, the forest's massed ranks in their silvery winter coats, delighted us with their depths. The mood on the sleighs was cheerful.

We looked for a suitable side road. By then it was broad daylight. The sun rose over the forest, its needle-like rays were shining on our faces by the time we went into the trees to get some rest. Soon we had a powerful bonfire flaring. The wood crackled joyfully and generously spread its warmth.

We heartily ate bread with pig's fat, smoked, discussed our impressions and made plans to see if we could contact the partisans. The main aim was to meet Bucko, their leader. Many of the partisans in this forest were supposed to be Jewish. My companions brought along a special gift for him — a square bottle of Passover spirits and a coat of otter fur for his daughter.

Around noon, fierce gunfire erupted about two kilometers away, surprising us. Machine guns, automatic weapons, single-action rifles and hand grenades were all being used. We had no idea where the shooting came from or the reason for it. Half an hour later, after it stopped, we heard movements of people on the forest road. Once, between the trees, we glimpsed gendarmes on sleighs hurrying out of the forest.

We were shocked. We loaded our guns and took up positions under the trees and waited. The tension lasted until the Germans were gone, running as if being chased. If they saw us, they ignored us. When night fell, three of us went in search of Bucko's home, a secluded farmhouse deep in the forest. We brought along the gifts.

The moon lit up the dense, frosty forest, casting a light blue glow on the snow, making it sparkle like ground glass. The sharpened steel runners whistled and squeaked in the crusty snow as the sleigh glided over it swiftly, like a little boat. The beautiful nocturnal landscapes stirred my imagination, and reminded me of sweet little children's stories from my youth.

We entered a broad white forest clearing in the middle of the forest that could have been a town square and made a right turn on the designated road. The horses ran at a gallop, hooves throwing clumps of snow up at us. We noticed a black spot on the snow-covered field that moved toward us. Guns at the ready, we slowed down and approached the human standing in front of us. It was a White Russian peasant woman with a walking stick in her hand.

We leaped from the sleigh and went up to her, peering at her face in the moonlight, when Shepsel and Beryl, my fellow travelers, jumped up and cried: "It's Bucko's wife!" and offered her their hands like old friends. The old woman recognized them and welcomed them back to her cottage.

"Ah, my children," she said joyfully, "I remember. You're from Grodno. You went off to bring more people with guns. Yes, yes, I remember."

My companions quickly brought her the fur coat and schnapps, wanting to please her. We were greatly surprised when she rejected the gifts and said quite clearly, "All we need is guns. These are foolish things."

When she saw our guns, she was very happy. She played with the gleaming revolvers in the moonlight like a child, constantly repeating, "Yes, this is what we need."

This simple White Russian peasant woman, who assessed the guns' great value in so manly a fashion, grew considerably in stature in my mind. She sat looking at the gleaming steel of the revolvers, beaming at them, admiring their beauty and murmuring continuously, "These precious things are what we need!"

She also told us that the Germans had attacked their small village that day. Her husband, Kostia, fled to the forest in time, but the Germans caught her brother-in-law, Sergey, and forced him, under threat of death, to show them the partisans' camp. Sergey had no choice and brought them to the forest. There were 13 gendarmes. He led them near the campsite, and advised them to fire into the air, which signaled the partisans, to come out of their bunkers. They would see the Germans and surrender.

The stupid Germans followed the peasant's "advice" and fired into the air, which alarmed the partisans, who understood the situation and welcomed the Germans with a healthy volley of gunfire. Sergey escaped in the commotion and six gendarmes were dead. The rest fled, taking their wounded with them, but they left behind six corpses, and gave the partisans their weapons, boots and furs. The old woman was thrilled that they had six more rifles, six Parabellums and many bullets.

She wished us a cordial farewell, asked where we were camped. She promised Kostia would most likely see us the following day. When we got back, we told our companions what happened. They sat around the campfire, stretching their hands toward the flames, and were thrilled that we would be meeting a leader who could declare us "citizens of the forest" and offer us "*lebensraum*" (Hitler's word for habitat or living space).

We dozed around the campfire, dreaming sweet dreams and hoping that the next day we would see the people whose marvelous exploits we had been hearing about in the ghetto — the legendary partisans.

The next morning, in the middle of February 1943, as we sat talking around the fire, a gigantic man, who looked as strong and sturdy as a pine tree, appeared as if from nowhere, carrying a semi-automatic weapon on his back.

"Here's Bucko," one of our companions called out. We all jumped up, ready to fling our arms around the neck of the White Russian partisan hero. He squeezed our hands in a friendly way and told us not to worry. "Everything will be fine," he comforted us in a fatherly manner. "Here you'll have the opportunity to get even with the enemy for the bloody injustice he's done you."

Out of gratitude, we filled his hat with bullets for his pistols. He was overjoyed, and smiled at his hat like a child. He read us the news from Soviet radio out of a notebook stowed in his inner coat pocket and asked if we had enough to eat. Later that night, he sent us a gift — Jewish partisans. There were two brothers, Chaim and Yankel Asner, Jews from the nearby Nacza, and Chaimke, a lad from Lida. They settled us in a safe location in the Radun Forest.

We treated the three young Jewish partisans travelling with us respectfully. We looked with envy at their German helmets, their white winter coats, felt boots and particularly the brand new guns, they captured the day before, in a battle with a German military unit. "May their hearts be sound," was how Chanan Elgin's old mother Tzivia, blessed them. "It's a pleasure to see how these bandits' clothes suit them."

"Don't worry, friends," the veteran partisans comforted us. "There's no lack of things to eat here. Tomorrow we'll teach you how to supply yourselves with food. Eventually you'll get guns and kill Germans as well as we do. The main thing is to live in peace among yourselves. Post a guard, and if you catch a stranger in the forest, let us know. We reckon that after the lesson we taught the Germans of Wasiliszki and Zablocie yesterday, they won't go crawling into the forest again."

Soon the horses left the forest path, "smuggling" themselves onto a little winding side path, running by a hand-cut forest clearing, and once again stealing into a little young forest — a sapling forest — and then the sleighs came to a halt.

"For the time being you'll sit here," said our three experienced partisans and gave us our first lesson in forest life. We broke off dry twigs and built a fire. The flames chased away the dark and warmed us up a little. The place was not far from the path that led to the villages of Sultaniszki, Soleczniki Wielki and Dubicze. The peasants in these villages were very poor and reacted to the partisans with sympathy.

The flames melted a large circle out of the snow and ice around it. We settled down, pulled off our shoes and boots, warmed our frozen feet, dried our wet clothes and had a bite to eat. In the distance, we could hear the howling of wolves sounding like a train's whistle. Protected by the trusty wings of the night, we all fell into a deep sleep.

Our teachers in the forest kingdom became our dear comrades: Michke Dubinski was an intelligent young man from Radun; Yankel Konichovski (a former worker-activist in pre-war Poland, who lived in Israel after the war) came from Woronów near Lida; Meyerke, a blacksmith from Radun carried rebellious traditions in his blood; Sholemke was a blacksmith from Zablocie near Wasiliszki - a good-natured middle-aged Jew. There were the four brothers Asner: Yankel, Avreymel, Chaim and Arke — from Nacza, and Yashke (the "Little Hand") — a metalworker from Radun — who distinguished himself in partisan battles. Leibel Katz — a former watchman from Olkieniki — was the adjutant to the Unit Commander.

There were others, as well. Our comrades led us through the dark nights via highways and byways, with guns in hand, and taught us how to supply ourselves with food. We went to faraway cottages and woke the peasants, who trembled like leaves. Scratching the backs of their heads, they pointed to their rich neighbors who'd "robbed enough Jewish blood," to offer us brandy and tobacco. They also offered to show us the way to "some Hasidic rabbi" who would surely provide for us.

In the morning we were on our feet again, alert to any sounds. The women fed us from a bucket of grits and meat from the calf we'd appropriated on our fourth day out of Grodno. Warm and well-fed, we made plans to take revenge on the Brown Shirts. We had a new German automatic pistol, a good Polish Browning, a small-caliber revolver (able to perforate a fat German) and a few dozen bullets. That was our temporary arsenal.

Suddenly a small sleigh appeared and two armed Russian partisans jumped out. They introduced themselves as the "Head of the Unit and Political Leader," and added jokingly, that they were "Masters of the Forest Kingdom." They greeted each of us cordially, asked if we had enough to eat, looked at our guns and conducted a transaction with us. Since we were not headed into the field for the time being, they would take our small arms and replace them with two rifles — Polish Mausers. We also gave them the German Parabellum.

We brought out the moonshine and drank to each other's health and to the speedy unnatural deaths of the Germans. Our guests told us radio reports said the Germans were defeated near Stalingrad, and gave us a breath of joy and hope. Before they left, they advised us to send scouts into the ghetto to see if there was anyone who could be rescued.

A few days later, Michke Dubinski, the partisan from Radun, and two of our brave comrades disguised themselves as peasants and went to Grodno to see if they could rescue any remaining Jews. Not far from Skidel they met a girl from Radun who'd escaped. She lied and said she was the last one left, so they put her in the sleigh and brought her to the forest. Later, we discovered her deception and were angry because we could have saved more people.

While sitting around the fire one day, we got a warning signal from the guard. He was holding a non-Jew who was wandering in the forest and we brought him in for interrogation. The young man claimed he wanted to join the partisans, but something was suspicious about the whole thing. Several people from the unit grilled him and discovered the Radun police had set him on our trail. His fate was sealed. When it became dark, his interrogators supposedly executed him. We were shocked when we got up the next morning, went to bury him and, instead of a corpse, found a bloody hat and tracks to the village. Obviously he had faked his death and was on his way to report. We had to move the campsite and do it quickly.

This was our first lesson as inexperienced partisans. We trudged through the snow until we found another hiding place. A friendly Polish partisan, Vintskovski from Radun, pointed the place out. We discovered a small earthen hut and some of our companions had a warm place for the night. The others slept around the campfire and often woke up with their clothes scorched.

One evening we harnessed one of the sleighs and went to the locals to get some food. We were still novices and didn't have enough guns to conduct open battles with the German gendarmes and their faithful dogs, the village police, so we took routes that avoided them. The feeling was mutual — the gendarmes didn't want to run into partisans, either.

But that night we were up against a brick wall. It was almost daybreak and somewhere a rooster crowed. We decided to spend the day in a peasant's farmhouse. When we knocked on his door, he shook himself awake and told us we were in Postawy not far from Ejszyzki. The peasant lit a fire, his wife offered us *blinis* with sour cream and we warmed our frozen bodies a little. Some of our companions fell asleep; some kept a watchful eye around the house. Our horse and sleigh were hidden in the cowshed. A few hours later, three peasants drove up. One of them was Bartsevitsh, headman of Nacza, who helped the Germans carry out pogroms on the few Jews in the village.

The Asner brothers had been looking for this bird for a long time. We spent a friendly day with him and made sure he wouldn't be able to escape. At night, when we said good-bye, we paid him back measure for measure. We shot the murderer like a dog on the snow-covered path. In his pocket we found a little torn Jewish prayer book. He was using its pages as toilet paper and to roll his cigarettes.

One day Dimitri Timofeyevitsh, the Unit Commander, told us he discovered a few solitary Jews in the forest and asked us to get to know them. We went with him and through the brush and trees, saw a bizarre image. A man with wildly overgrown black hair, his feet wrapped with rags, was squatting on the ground next to a smoldering fire. Next to him were two children, a boy and a girl, both about 13 years old. There was a little tabernacle, braided from twigs, their "forest palace."

We frightened him, but soon he told us in a trembling, choked voice that his name was Yeshaye. He was a tailor from Marcinkonys. During the last slaughter in the *shtetl*, several Jewish families ran to the forest, built a little house for themselves and hoped to survive. Many of them had money and bought food from the surrounding peasants. But one morning they were attacked by the Semashkos, a rich peasant family from Kowel, who lined up at the door of their cottage and shot the Jews one by one, including his wife and one of his children.

He, his son and a girl who was Tzemach the Baker's daughter from Grodno were somehow spared and trudged barefoot through the snow for several kilometers, until they found safe haven on that very spot. An acquaintance, a rural Christian woman, secretly brought them a few potatoes and some bread from time to time. Then Yeshaye showed us a pit, partly covered by twigs with two corpses inside — two youths from Grodno (one of them was Krenitse from Grandzic Street). The youths escaped from the Grodno ghetto and built a little bunker. One cold evening they brought a few glowing coals into the bunker for warmth and covered the entrance. They fell asleep and died from coal gas. Their terribly swollen faces looked toward us, frozen, as if asking us to bury them. We did. When we were done, Yeshaye sat with us, freshly washed and shaven, and with a piece of meat in his hand, announced, "I'll be your tailor!"

Not far from us was a camp with Jews from Radun. They were known as "Elik's group," named for Elik, a village peddler who knew the forest well. Before the slaughter in Radun, he went into the forest with his family, built bunkers with stoves and doors and made plank beds to sleep on. He had enough to eat and kept to himself, and did not want us hanging around as guests.

Spring was coming. The snow gradually disappeared, the trees got back their greenery and we walked on forest moss that carpeted the earth. Our forest family began to grow. About a dozen young people escaped from the Lida ghetto and joined us. They brought along sawed-off shotguns, hand grenades and bullets stolen from German depots. There were two doctors with them — Dr. Rubinstein and his wife Lucia (who moved to Israel after the war), and a woman doctor from Leningrad with her 4-year-old daughter. She was the senior doctor at the Jewish hospital in Grodno, and during the first few days of the German invasion helped that captured Jewish airman, Lifshits, escape. The Gestapo was hunting for her when she escaped to Lida and from there to our place in the forest.

The Lida companions went back to Lida to save more Jews and brought them to the forest. One of the people who joined them was the teacher, Yudel Raiskind from Grodno (a son of the owner of the sanitation works on Grandzic Street), but he was murdered by the Polish AK [Armija Krajowa; Home Army].

One evening Avreymel Pave, Leizer Sisun, Pinye Mazavyetski, Beryl Lipski (the shoemaker), Yerachmiel, a young man from Olkieniki, and Yanek, a partisan from Radun, set out to get some food and put out feelers to see which peasants had guns. They went about 10 kilometers from our place. The fellows were young and brave, with little experience, but they never came back. The next day our messengers learned that the Radun police were on their trail, surrounded the cottage where they were for the day and opened fire on them. The men under attack defended themselves to the last bullet and died when the police set fire to the cottage. Pinye Mazavyetski managed to grab a horse and escaped. But they pursued him for several kilometers and shot him. We were never able to find out who the informer was, and the blood that was shed remained unavenged.

One day a new group of Jews from Grodno came to us. They were Mrs. Berezovski (who owned the tar factory) and her two small boys; Lisa Munaker, an intelligent woman; Itshke Goldrey, who owned a carpenter's shop and was a son of Leibe Gratsh; a wagon driver, Yankel Magadavski (called Yankel Fishke's), and a young woman, Rita (the granddaughter of R. Shimon Shkap, the Rosh Yeshiva in Grodno). They were the last Jews of Grodno.

Our forest family grew to 80 people. It was difficult and dangerous to be on the move with such a defenseless crowd. Often we would catch suspicious characters in our area and realized they were informers. They paid for their crimes. We were aware the district gendarmes were interested in us. There were about 70 Jews from Lida half a kilometer from us, many of them women and children. Elik's group was four kilometers further away and it had grown to 60 people.

The good-natured commander of the unit, Lieutenant Stankiewicz, was our guest almost daily. Our youngsters would ask him to include them in the unit and give them the opportunity to take revenge. But guns were hard to get. Stankiewicz's unit of almost 200 people operated on a large scale. His group cut the enemy the deepest with their sabotage operations. Stankiewicz, who was in his 20s, held political office in Skidel before the war. He sent 10 Jewish men to Vilna to save a couple of Jews. Unfortunately only a few of them came back.

Little by little, many of the Jews from Grodno were inducted into the unit and brought much honor to the Jewish people with their heroism. They were Beryl Lipski; Shepsel Garbulski, and Yankel Magadavski (Yankel Fishke's) who was a machine gunner and killed many Germans, but he died tragically in Radun after the liberation. Yankel Gratsh, a graduate of the Tsisho School, was an excellent shot in the "Perekap" unit near Slonim and died in one of the battles.

Avrom Kapulski and his 15-year-old son Hirshele were heroes, too. Kapulski senior died in battle and the young Hirshele took vengeance on the Germans, despite his age (he lived in Canada after the war); Moishe Kayles and Shloime and Velvl Pave died in battle, sacrificing their young lives for the freedom of all of us.

CHAPTER 17

Conclusion of the Scroll of Nacza

About 5,000 Germans, Lithuanians, peasant police and other Nazi collaborators surrounded the Nacza Forest in mid-June 1943. Captured Jews were tortured and killed. A few managed to hide themselves in the bushes and then moved to other forests. Some in the Lida group ran back to the ghetto and ended their lives in gas chambers or mass graves. The Angel of Death reaped a rich harvest in Nacza Forest that day.

Several days later, a few survivors went back to find and bury the corpses. Among the murdered Jews I found my good friends the brothers Peyshke and Leibl Manes and Rive, the doctor from the Jewish hospital and her 4-year-old daughter Chayaleh. Most of the people killed were from Elik's group. They had been chased through marshlands and found their last resting-place in the mud of the Stayer Forest.

The stench of rotting corpses, carried by the wind, led us to them. We gathered them in homespun bed sheets, little bone to little bone and dug a mass grave in a dry place. Someone cut a piece of bark from a birch tree above head height with a sharp knife and wrote on the trunk with a pencil, "Here lay innocent Jews murdered by German bandits. Honor their memory. Eternal vengeance." One Jew said *Kaddish*, and the echo of our *Amen* carried far into the old forest.

A few weeks later, Michke from Radun, Yashke the "Little Hand," and a third partisan carried out acts of vengeance. They blew up a German military train at the Tsherlana station near Lunną destroyed twelve Tiger tanks and more than twenty Ferdinands. They killed about 100 Germans in the process. Stankiewicz promised to award medals to the three courageous partisans after the liberation.

Only a few small groups of Jews remained in Nacza Forest after the police raid. They were terrorized by the newly-created pro-Fascist Polish-Lithuanian gangs, like the "A.K.," "N.S.Z." and other armed groups. In this dangerous situation, the unit had to move continually. Some of the Grodno partisans were posted to the forests of Lipiczansk by the Nieman River, others nearer to Slonim, by the Szczara river.

The unit concentrated all its activity on destroying the pro-Nazi gangs. After a battle near Kowel several fascists were killed, so the gangs attacked the unit the next day and murdered one of its mainstays, our savior Kostia Bucko and his whole family, as well as a large number of partisans. Only a limited number of people managed to save themselves. Frumke, Bashele and I were among them.

At the end of August 1943, it was no longer possible to stay in the Nacza Forest, and we, a very small group of partisans, set off one summer evening to wander down dark forest paths, further away, to a safer partisan zone, nearer the banks of the Nieman River.

CHAPTER 18

Life in the Forest

Slowly the sun, a powerfully glowing red ball, set in the west, and with its last rays it lit up our safe haven near Feremak not far from Marcinkonys. It was a level forest area, where the borders of Russia, Poland and Lithuania met. We were on the Polish side, about one and a half kilometers from a German garrison.

We said good-bye to our comrades from the Leninsky Komsomol partisan unit and set off with a small group of scouts, who were traveling to headquarters in Bakszty. It was really hard to say good-bye to so many good people and especially to Commander Stankiewicz — who defensively repeated over and over again, "Well, you know yourself that you can't be in a unit with a 6-year-old child. The enemy is treading on our toes, and our tactics are to give him a pinch and make a fast getaway. Go to the Nieman River — there's a large partisan zone there — and after the liberation we'll surely meet again."

While speaking he entered the staff booth and brought out my rifle. "Take the rifle. You've got a family. It could come in handy." When people headed east, the local partisans usually confiscated their weapons. The partisans in the east were supplied by regular Soviet air drops.

The good-natured Stankiewicz loved my little daughter and called her *Tshornoglazka* (black-eyed girl), and would very often bring her gifts. The life of the forest was difficult. One always had to keep eyes wide open like an animal on the alert. The only moral satisfaction came from beating down the hated enemy and listening to the news from the front on the radio. We slept in our clothes and didn't take our boots off for months at a time. Yet the stress seemed not to have at all damaged Stankiewicz, a noble, scarcely more than 20-year-old Russian. Perhaps in his heart he longed for his own child and young wife, who were wandering in the forests and villages near Skidel.

We were now a group of 10, who quickly walked on narrow paths and byways between the aging pine trees toward Zablocie. We knew we would have to detour around it in the middle of the night because of its vigilant police garrison. Suddenly, heavy, dense clouds appeared above the tree tops and wiped the stars from the sky, delighting us because it was going to be a dark night. Soon it began to pour by the proverbial bucket load. We welcomed the rain because as homeless Jews trying to save themselves, there were fewer risks of being discovered when it rained.

Our baggage, which consisted of a woolen blanket, a loaf of black bread and the clothes on our backs, became much heavier in the rain. But what did it matter? We were walking in hope of living and finding much yearned-for freedom. Six-year-old Basheleh conducted herself bravely. Her little bare feet stepped on sharp pine needles and little pebbles, and she even stubbed her toes against a tree stump. Instead of crying, she bit her lips, groaned and hopped around a little bit. She knew that one was not supposed to cry.

We had a stretch of almost a hundred kilometers ahead of us. We walked in the direction of the Nieman River, which meandered toward Bielica and Jeloudok (Jołudek) and formed a large semi-circle through Lunna, Mosty and Grodno, toward Druskieniki. This wooded area was home to many partisans.

Around midnight, we detoured around Zablocie, as expected. In the distance, rockets rose into the air, brightly lit up the area and slowly fell to the ground in a semi-circle. With each rocket, we huddled on the ground, motionless. When it was clear, we moved quickly forward until the next rocket went up. We did that to avoid enemy eyes and bullets. When the attacks were over, we dragged ourselves through the mud to a row of poor cottages, known as "stripes," and knocked at the door of a friendly White Russian peasant. He opened the door and was genuinely pleased to see us.

He filled a trough with warm water and was willing to stand there and wash the dirty rags from our feet. Our boots were long gone. Frumke and Bashele were asleep on the warm stove, snoring heartily. I was soon lying on the stove, too, battling a plague of fleas that literally tore pieces of flesh from our bodies.

In the morning, the kind-hearted Andrei, a non-Jew, took us to a small dense birch wood a few hundred meters from his cottage, and to our great joy, united us with a group of comrades who escaped the Nazi raid on the Nacza Forest. We were delighted to see each other alive. In no time, there was a pot of lamb stew on the fire. They gave us small pieces of black bread the size of olives and satisfied our hunger.

Our group now consisted of about 20 souls. They were Sholem-Meyer Kanapke (a middle-aged gardener from Lida); Lyuvsik Voltshinski and his wife Chana from Wasiliszki (they moved to Israel after the war); Big Syomek from Zablocie and his wife Tsipele, from Vilna; Moishke Zablatski (a peddler from Zablocie, and his wife; Sholem-Lev, also from Zablocie, and his two cousins, the Krażevskis from Lida).

Yerachmiel Portnoy from Wasiliszki (who later moved to Israel) was a spiteful individual and did nothing but needle me. He kept asking, "Why on earth do you want to save your wife and child, when I let my own die?" He constantly incited our companions to mutiny so that I would desert Bashele and Frumke. He would say,"The impudence of the person! To drag such a child along!"

There were also several escaped prisoners of war, former Soviet soldiers.

Our journey was still dangerous. We marched at night and hid during the day because we were surrounded by Polish villages with wealthy peasants who had watchful eyes, and where the Fascist N.S.Z. and the A.K. were lying in wait.

We added distance and time when we had to crawl across plowed fields and find back roads to avoid meeting well-armed murderers. Most were ex-officers, policemen and other lackeys, rich Polish landowners, who lived in peace with the cruel occupiers who drowned their land in blood.

We walked for three nights, and when dawn broke on the fourth morning, we were at the banks of the Nieman River in the White Russian village of Zblyan, between Bielica and Żołudek. Somewhere along the opposite bank of the river there was a dense green forest which called to us. We stood at the banks of the Nieman River, and our thoughts went back to the past, when the same river bore witness to the lost freedom of our youth, as well as its bloodiest conclusion.

I didn't know a soul who hadn't bathed in the ample waves of the familiar river. Everyone remembered all the places where the Jewish youth of Grodno would meet to have fun.

I felt like prostrating myself and kissing the soil on the banks of this dear river and sent a heartfelt greeting to the tormented, extinct Jews of Grodno along its flowing currents. The now Jewless city was once the "city and mother of Israel." But there was no time for romanticism or sentiment. It was August 1943, and the enemy was tearing the Jews out by their roots. Here and there were flickering sparks of surviving Jews. Several kept on struggling right there at the banks of the Nieman.

Our comrade woke up a boatman who sleepily untied his small boat and ferried us to the other side. We stepped into a deep, green carpet of grass in a dense pine forest, and knew that above all we were on friendly soil in a large partisan zone. Soon we met Jewish partisans, fighters in the Orlianski Unit founded by Jews from Orlia further down the Nieman River.

We were greeted by good-natured, neighborly Jews who were fit and who were once residents of Zhetl (Żdzięcioł; Diatlovo), Szczuczyn, Bielica, Zołudek, Lida, Nowogródek, Baranowicze, Nowojelina and other towns and *shtetls*. They carried machine guns and were wrapped in bandoliers filled with bullets. They were simple Jews: artisans, wagon drivers, farmers, fearless lads and girls, who took pride in their marksmanship and the honor of being the avengers of their annihilated families. Among them were modest heroes who did not speak of their own achievements.

The older partisans were delighted to see us and quizzed us, as is the Jewish custom. Where did we come from? Where had we been? When they got our precise replies, they brought cheese and sour cream down from the wagons, crumbled it in a large clay bowl and mixed it together, cut small slices of fresh black bread, and brought out some homemade schnapps. We drank to each other's health, sat down on the green moss and shared a celebratory meal among friends. The group of people we found were the unit's suppliers, and they had just returned from night operations.

Jews from family groups with wives and children lived in the nearby forest and moved about the supply wagons as if it was market day. They traded with their Jewish partisan brothers — shoe soles for flour, home-brewed schnapps for clothing and other such deals.

The forest we were in was called "Karashuker Forest," after the nearby

White Russian village, where there were about 80 Jews, mostly from Bielica. They hid in small groups scattered through the trees.

It was not easy to approach and join these groups. Just as corrupt and bad people can become good and kind in easy times, in dangerous times, good people can sometimes become corrupt and selfish. Several days passed while we sat in the brush and wondered how we could get some help. Who would take an interest in us? Who would want to "adopt" us and teach us the secrets of this new forest? How and where could we get bread?

Two Jews who looked like real White Russian peasants and were barefoot, came to see us. They talked to us for bit and, sensing that we were truly Jewish, asked us to come with them if we didn't want to be on our own. We wanted to fling our arms around their necks in deep gratitude for their kindheartedness. These were two Jews from Bielica, Herzl Fleisher and Mulye Shimenovitch, both former inkeepers in that *shtetl*. (The former went off to Israel later, together with his brother Yaakov and sister Chaiki, and the latter moved to Baltimore, Maryland, USA with his wife and four children.)

After a 30-minute walk through the woods, we found 15 people sitting around a fire in a birch wood. There was Mulye with six family members, Herzl and his family of four and another five people. Frumke, Bashele and I added three more people. We were now part of a new forest family.

We pulled out a coarse bedsheet to use as a roof underneath a dense pine tree and put down our "bag of sorrows" to use as a pillow. I put the rifle to one side and we rested our tired, bruised bones. We quickly adapted to living together with the new Jews and became "one soul" with them. They were kind-hearted people with spirit. Mulye's two sons, Hershel and Shimon, and his two daughters, Kune and Reyze, were well-brought-up and shared their crusts of bread with us.

They taught us the unfamiliar routes, never lost their courage, always showed a real, youthful, healthy energy and were sure that we would survive. Mulye was a modern, intelligent Jew and a great prankster. He cheered up our forest family and provoked laughter until we cried.

He and many other captured Jews were once lined up for execution at a wall by the Germans, who shot them at point blank range. He told us he survived by making himself fall with those who were executed, as if he too had died. When the opportune moment arrived, like a miracle from above, he vanished from the place of slaughter. His wife, Tsherne-Bayla, stood tirelessly at the fire for entire days, cooking special dishes for the little children, as if she was in her own home. She made *kishka* — stuffed derma, *p'tcha* — calf's foot in aspic, *schmaltz* dumplings and other delicious treats.

Herzl Fleisher, his brothers Yankel and Leishke (who later died in the forest) and his sister Chaike, were all dedicated, special people. When they were forced to flee their homes, the men wanted to take only their prayer shawls and phylacteries, which they guarded like the eyes in their heads. They didn't cook or smoke on *Shabbes*, and in general tried to keep *Shabbes* properly. Leishke was once a yeshiva student who knew many rabbinic tales and stories from Yiddish folk literature. When we had time to sit around the fire, he entertained us by telling us his stories.

Things were relatively quiet for a couple of months, and when winter approached, we built bunkers with little stoves in the walls made from bricks salvaged from burned-out cottages in the forest. We were delightfully warm and comfortable. We even baked bread. On *Shabbes* we visited other Jews living with their wives and children a few kilometers away from us. They would offer us *cholent* and *kugel*, while vehemently cursing Hitler, may his name be blotted out.

The Jews from Bielica learned the art of building hiding-places in the forest. New Year's 1944 quickly approached. Our small group sat in our snow-covered bunkers with our small supply of food. Frequent visitors were forest birds and "Reb Wolfy," who sneaked in at night and would pinch whatever was left outside. Because we didn't want to leave tracks in the snow, we went to the villages as little as possible,

A unit of fascist Russian turncoats and Nazi collaborators, followers of Lieutenant General Andrei Vlasov, advanced on our area. The huge defeats in the east forced the enemy to try to clear the area of partisans. The partisans continued to inflict serious damage and prepared a safe retreat if they had to run.

The noose tightened and before we knew it the Vlasovites were right under our noses. We had to leave our warm nests and drag ourselves 20 kilometers deeper into the woods, dragging our bundles and ourselves in the middle of winter, through burning frost and long dark forest corridors. We went as far as the Lipiczansk Forest, where there was a main base for many partisan divisions — whose good will allowed the Jews to survive.

Frozen and exhausted, we arrived at a Jewish partisans' camp in the middle of the night. I knocked at the door of a bunker and someone let us in. A delightful warmth caressed our frozen limbs. We were in a pitch-dark room, but slowly our eyes adjusted and we could see the outlines of figures sitting on their plank beds.

Then a woman's voice asked, "Jews, who are you?"

"We are Grodno Jews," I answered.

"Oh, Grodno Jews," she said, and remained silent. We realized that we chanced upon our own people. Our hostess, Lisa Garber, was a well-known actress in Grodno who was married to Leib Kovenski, a forester from Zhetl, who knew the large forest well. He'd moved his family from Zhetl to escape death. Lisa's sister-in-law, Shmuel Garber's wife, had her partisan son Avreymel with her.

Before the war, Shmuel Garber was editor of the magazine *Grodner Lebn* ("Grodno Life") and was an acquaintance of mine. When the war began, he went off to Zhetl with his family, and was one of the first to set up the Orlianski Unit, where he served as a medic. The great intellectual was felled by the Nazi beasts at the beginning of 1943. (May these few words serve as an epitaph).

The widow of my murdered friend recognized my voice at once and was overjoyed that my family was still alive. She lit a small piece of kindling and prepared a warm place by the stove where we could sleep. In the dim light cast by the kindling, we counted about nine individuals, half-sitting on their plank beds, all belonging to one and the same family, looking with pitying glances at us, the homeless fugitives and wanderers. Their joy at being able to share their living space with us was clear.

The next few months were quiet, and we spent it peacefully among ourselves. Living in the forest camp with the Jews from Zhetl and Grodno felt like living in a small *shtetl*. The only things missing were the bathhouse and the house of study, a *Beis Medrash*. The camp consisted of about a dozen bunkers filled with people from Zhetl who did not lose their sense of humanity even in such cruel times.

There were two other similar camps a few kilometers further away, where other Jews from Zhetl found safe haven. All told, there were about a hundred individuals in the forest. Often partisans came to us and gave us their clothes to mend. Lisa also made underwear for them, out of recycled parachute silk. She even had a sewing machine in her forest cottage. The partisans paid for the services they received with meat, cooking fat, butter, cheese, flour and even a few bottles of alcohol.

About that time, we saw that senior officers from the Polish army were being parachuted into the forest and were recruiting civilians, similar to our partisans, who would be assigned special tasks. The airplanes would ride low over the forest and drop cases of guns, ammunition and medicines for the partisans. When they could land, they took the severely injured away with them.

We sensed that the enemy's end was fast approaching, and we also felt spring in the air, but still had to be quite careful, because the enemy was moving closer to us as they retreated. Jews were still Public Enemy Number One, even though the murderers were well and truly battered and on the road home. They continued killing and murdering as they went. And then, one fine sunny June morning, the radio announced the happy news that the Allies had landed their armies in France.

Until that very day, Vlasov's murderers, Hitler's vassals, had planted mines and began their offensive against our part of the forest. Shrapnel whistled over the tree tops, branches creaked and splinters rained like hail. Machine guns incessantly did their work, and once again, we had to leave our huts and hide in previously prepared hideouts.

These secret bunkers, prepared by the Jews in case of trouble, were architectural wonders that could only have been invented by people seeking to escape the Angel of Death. They were long underground corridors with a concealed entrance hidden by bushes or a forest spring. Ventilation shafts were hidden in the roots of the trees. We crawled through these corridors on all fours, until we reached a larger and higher "room," built of dry, thick reeds, with a little water well in it, food supplies and other essentials.

Usually, the Jews built their caves in family units, and kept them secret, having suffered bitter experiences in the ghettos, where other Jews became informers who revealed hiding places because they were envious. Frumke, Bashele and I ran from the Janowice Forest to the Earl's Forest, where Lyusik Wolczynski, a young man from Wasiliszki, a friend of mine, was hiding with his wife Chana. He'd promised that in time of danger he would share his cave with us. Frumke and I became good friends with this amiable couple in the Nacza Forest. To get to his hiding place, we needed to cover several kilometers in the bright, hot, sun. We left behind our bundles of clothes, underwear and a few other essentials.

When we got there, we found that Wolczynski needed help finishing the bunker. So we helped him out, working like demons beneath a hail of bullets. We cut down little trees, thatched a roof of forest grass, pine needles and cones and fashioned an entrance beneath a fallen tree. When we finished, we slipped into the hollow, which measured one and a half meters by three and a half meters. There were 15 of us. We lay there exhausted, drained of our strength, with our ears tuned to the forest noises and our nerves on the edge of shattering. We heard every creak above us.

The roar of the rockets got closer. When they were launched, they whistled like birds, but by the time they came down, they finished with frightful howling as they burst. It was terribly demonic death music.

When night fell, we crawled out of our caves to find out what was going on and to see if anyone had been hurt or worse, God forbid. It also gave us a chance to breathe a little cool, fresh air. Jews lit fires in the abandoned bunkers, frying potatoes or boiling them for the next day. When dawn broke, they disappeared.

The Vlasovites had set up their headquarters only a kilometer away from us. We could even feel the vibration of their footsteps above us. One night several airplanes flew over us. We could tell they were friendly from the sound of their engines. They dropped flares above us and, produced beautiful illumination of the entire area. At the same time, they dropped a hail of bombs on the Vlasovites' headquarters. That night brought us such joy as cannot be imagined. Even the greatest skeptics finally believed redemption was near.

Food was hard to get because the Vlasovites, like wolves, ambushed the Jews in the brush and sadistically murdered them. On quieter days we went to the forest meadow where there were masses of wild strawberries, berries and mushrooms that we gathered for sustenance.

Then one night we heard cannon shots nearby, and in the morning, heard, to our indescribable joy, that Baranowicze had been liberated and that the Brown-Shirted two-legged beasts had abandoned Nowogródek as well.

We eagerly waited for the arrival of our redeemers. The Vlasovites crept about in the forest, wearing their German uniforms, asking us to take them prisoner and not to kill them. They claimed that the Germans forced them to do their dirty work — to murder the Jews. First the partisans took away their arms, and then they meted out the justice of the forest.

On the July 9, 1944, at dusk, we heard motor vehicles on the forest path and despite the darkness noticed familiar insignia on the cars. The redeemers had arrived. Such moments cannot be expressed in words, and still less described on paper. One can only feel them if they had been condemned to death and liberated through a miracle. Old and young people, grown-ups and children, men and women, hugged one another and pressed each other to their hearts.

In Antshari, headquarters had been set up at the mill, where the artillery general, an older man, ordered his men to give us food from their kitchen. He had his photograph taken with us — a few dozen Jews. The guards tenderly caressed our children, as if smoothing away the great and cruel wrong inflicted on our innocent, unfortunate people.

CHAPTER 19

Freedom

It was July 8 or 9 1944, The forest road wound its way parallel to the Nieman River to Grodno, 120 kilometers away. We were camped between Lida and Nowogródek, two kilometers from the small White Russian village Demyonovtse, which was on the sandy shores of the Nieman.

It was almost impossible to believe that we had survived the onslaught; that we were free and could safely go back to our towns, and no one would bother us. Going home was an eerie experience. Planes with red stars on their wings hummed brightly, flying low, reinforcing the feeling in our hearts that those pirate's airplanes with the crosses on their wings had finally disappeared and we were safe walking on the highway. We were dressed in rags, exhausted from the last hard month before liberation. Vlasovites blockaded our forest area with tens of thousands of men, and hardly let us breathe. "Who knows?" the forest Jews had declared with one voice, "If the Red Army had been delayed a few more days, would any of us have survived?

The front was moving steadily westward. The Germans ran like mice from the Red Army and from the "music" of Russian "Katyushas".

In Bielica, we had the good fortune to guard a camp of German prisoners of war — soldiers and senior officers. These human beasts looked at us with their dull, stupid faces and could not imagine where Jewish civilians had come from, especially with rifles in hand. A captured colonel wanted to check things out and asked me: "You speak German well. Are you an ethnic German?"

"No!" I shouted and with spite added, "We are Jews, my comrades and I, risen from the grave. And we'll pay back Hitler's dogs many times over." He lowered his stupid face and said nothing more.

On July 17, 1944, Grodno was liberated. From Skidel, there is a 32 kilometer twisting mountain road that leads to the city. Usually it is a 45-minute drive by car. But this time the journey was slow. The truck from Bielica to Grodno was heavily loaded with ammunition and was making sluggish progress. Frumke, my now 8-year-old Bashele, and I were on board.

And yet how strange. I would not have minded traveling like this for a long time, so as not to arrive too quickly. Once I got there I was afraid of what I would find, and not find. I was sure I wasn't going to find anybody, and would surely not meet anyone I used to know. And yet uncertainties tormented me and I tried to console myself--perhaps this one or that one survived — a distant cousin, a chance meeting? Could it really be that more than 25,000 Jews from Grodno were annihilated root and branch?

The car made a sharp turn to the right and on the horizon the top of the Słobodka orphanage tower, church crosses, factory chimneys and the tower of the water works were all visible. I saw my Grodno laid out as if on the back of my hand.

There was Słobodka, where Ghetto No. 2 once stood. There was no longer any barbed wire fence, but fence posts were still stood here and there. The gateway guardhouse (at the corner of Fik's barracks) was spitefully intact, sad witness to the recent past. The emptiness of the big orphanage frightened me. I could almost hear the screams of the last orphans being dragged away.

I lurked about, all eyes, brushing each passer-by with my glance. They were all strangers, complete strangers. It seemed to me I had never set eyes on any of them before. They were all well-dressed, as if in their Sunday best, though it was only a weekday. And I could swear their clothing had all been originally cut to Jewish taste. Many passers-by looked at us with great surprise: Some great news! There were a few Jews in Grodno!

An individual with a round, pimply face was bold enough to put his fleshy, sweaty hand toward me, a dead-alive Jew, like an old acquaintance. And in a poisonously ingratiating way, he asked, *"Jak się masz?"* (How do you do?) The hand of this unknown "friend," whose face and clothes testified that he had been closely connected to our misfortune, scorched me. I pulled my own hand back and turned away in contempt. From familiar windows on the first and second floor of the building I used to live in, unknown faces stared at us with curious eyes that held no pity.

It was eerie to walk through the once familiar but now completely strange, streets. A wealthy Pole, an old acquaintance of ours, who for years, had worked with my father, Frumke and with me at Lapin's, the lithographer, was "somewhat happy" to see us and prepared a "roomy" place for us to sleep on his kitchen floor. His wife, an old, pious Christian, was very worried and grumbled that it was too much to help us. I assured her we would leave the next morning. She was so delighted we would be gone. She gave Bashele a plate of grits. My wife sobbed quietly, tossing and turning on the hard floor, and I wracked my brains to figure out how to put a roof over our heads the following morning.

The Polish woman who lived in my ghetto apartment (36 Troytse Street) was surprised and enraged at my "impudence" for demanding my apartment back. She ran off to report the crime to the town commander. He summoned us, looked at us for a moment and told the Polish woman to give back the apartment.

Nearly 15,000 Jews had been jammed together in Ghetto No. 1, in the courtyard of the synagogue and the fish market. That part of town, which had always been Jewish, looked like a cemetery. A devilish hand had thrown down all the little wooden houses and left only heaps of rubble and bricks. Bigger buildings remained standing, empty and ruined, with no doors or windows, the empty spaces stared into the distance like blind eyes.

Mezzuzot on door lintels testified that Jews had once lived there. In the ruined, looted apartments, Jewish religious books, secular books and journals were tossed around on the floors. Here and there we found photographs with familiar faces crying out from the floors of abandoned homes.

The beautiful butchers' synagogue, where I spent my earliest youth, was empty and hollow. A vandal's hand had smashed the exceptionally beautiful ark. A Yiddish inscription on the door caught my eye, "You are asked not to spit or hawk on the floor." I read the same words again and again and remained standing frozen for a moment, as if I wanted to pay my respects to the last Jewish inscription in a Jewish town.

The brick wall of the old cemetery had collapsed. I once played there during the happy days of my youth. I knew every stone and heard many stories about martyrdom in sanctification of God's name. Each headstone evoked much holy terror in my child's soul. In the time of the ghetto, large mass graves were dug there because of the frequent killings in the ghetto. Now it was difficult to find any trace of the graves. There were heaps of rubbish everywhere. Pragmatic Christians, who lived in Jewish apartments, fenced off small portions of the field with various boards and some old tin sheets, to let their pigs graze there.

A Christian fireman told me: "The patients who were lying in the ghetto hospital were shot after the liquidation of the ghetto by the murderer Kurt Wiese. He ordered the last surviving Jew to throw the dead into the lime pit, opposite the big *Beis Medrash* in Gershon Menaker's — the butcher's--courtyard." The story was credible, because near the pit was the wall where Wiese used to line up the captured, even after the liquidation. The Roman Catholics used it as a garbage dump, and religiously dumped their trash on Jewish graves every day.

It was a hot summer. The ground in the cemetery began to settle, but my efforts to exhume the holy martyrs from their mass graves came to nothing (for health reasons), and there was no one to help me. The new cemetery on Grandzic Street was also ruined and desecrated. During the time of the occupation, the hooligan masters of the town took the headstones from more than half of the cemetery to build staircases and sidewalks. Peasants hammered millstones out of them to grind corn for their own use.

Leib Naidus's impressive grave marker remained standing. But at first glance, it seemed that the weeping angel bowed his head deeper and lower to the ground. The marker on the grave of the revolutionary Dovid Skultshik, who died in Grodno prison while on a hunger strike on August 14, 1931, also survived the sinister power of fascism and threatened the world with its revolutionary inscription.

At my mother's grave I found broken pieces of her headstone. Bit by bit I put the pieces back on the grave and chased away some cows grazing nearby. I said good-bye to my mother's grave and Frumke, Bashele and I left the town of Grodno — where people could not find peace after death — forever.

AFTERWORD

by Betty (Reizer) Broit

Dad started writing his memoirs just after the war while we were still in the DP camps in Austria and Germany. He finished it in 1948 when we arrived in New Zealand where he had an older brother.

He believed that it was his moral duty to write his story because he felt "that it is a crime to keep quiet and not tell of the dark times in all its phases." When referring to the manuscript he would write:

> I was careful and honest with every word, so that God forbid there should be no gossip leading to some Jews being wronged. I think it is of the utmost importance to write about everything in the purest truth, not to hide anything or beautify ugly deeds of some Jews who had deceitful and harmful attitudes and the bloodiest of interest for our brothers, and who perhaps thought by these means that they could save themselves — ended up only being traitors to their own people.... Don't be shocked by my introduction where I describe a bit of my personal pain and experience during the time when I ran away from Grodno to Minsk. This was not characteristic of me personally. Many, many Jews made that same journey.
>
> You should not think that my memoirs contain an excess of sadness and that I am trying to paint our past in overly tragic colors. I tell it as a simple human being, a man who can write a Yiddish

letter, a man with a clear conscience, and one who did not exaggerate in describing the activities and tactics of the Judenrat and their faithful servants the ghetto police....

While we were in the DP camps he kept himself occupied by taking an active part in the cultural life there. In Bindermichl, for instance, under his initiative, a drama group was formed named for Shalom Aleichem. The performances were well received by the large audience of the camp that hungered for the Yiddish word and Yiddish theater.

After presenting five successful shows they took the plays and revues to Salzburg and Bad Ischl. The continuous applause indicated the audience's enjoyment. The three items on that particular program were: "Der Nes" written by Dad — a light hearted cheerful comedy which was a reflection of our wanderings, "A 66", and "Olam Haba", both by Shalom Aleichem.

In the year we spent in the DP camp Geretsried while waiting for our papers to come through for New Zealand he was taking part in communal work, especially in helping to form a school and a kindergarten there, and from time to time bring out a Yiddish theater. He used to say that "if a serious theater did happen to find its way to Geretsried the prices were so steep that the audience remembered the prices much longer than the show itself..."

In May 1948 we finally arrived in New Zealand, and by then there was an addition to the family — my sister Judy, who was born in Lodz in 1945.

In an obituary for his older brother Nissan, Dad wrote:

> After a separation of 28 years the two brothers met. I looked older than my brother. I was gray, with a wrinkled face and the fear in my eyes had not yet vanished. It was wintertime when I arrived in the far away country. And there I found that the trees were green, flowers bloomed, and the sun with its gentle rays was caressing my grey head and aged face. I inhaled the fresh air, looked at the green fields with its abundant white sheep and after the destruction of Europe I found myself enveloped in a happy contentment.[5]

5 *Grodner Opklangen* 16, June 1966. *Grodner Opklangen* was a Yiddish newspaper published in Argentina until 1980.

Dad had left the hell of Europe and arrived in paradise ...

Dad was born in 1910. He was the second youngest of eight children (Israel, Dina, Nissan, Shlomo, Avram, Yehoshua, Leib and Miriam) and came from a traditional religious Zionist home. Out of the eight children born to his parents Note and Basia, four (Nissan, Yehoshua, Avram and Miriam) made aliya to Israel between the years 1920 and mid-1930. One of them, Yehoshua, drowned while swimming in the Haifa Bay in 1928.

Dad was the only one in the family who had a more "socialist" political leaning. He grew up at a time when politically-oriented thinking youth were striving and planning on how to build a better world, a world of freedom and justice for all. The groups would meet in his beloved forests around Grodno and speakers would lecture and explain to the young workers all about the structure of society and its social and economic laws, pointing out various ways of fighting for a just order. They hammered into those young minds the ideas of freedom and lit a flame in their hearts and a belief in a bright future. And as he told us children many years later, it did not take him long "to see the light" and become disenchanted at a very early stage with the ideology.

Dad was very modest, to the point where he did not mention that the whole time we were in the Nacza Forest he was appointed Elder of a group of eighty people by the commander of the partisan unit "Leninski Komsamol." He hated inflated egos and formality in any form and felt uncomfortable in a stiff "English environment". I remember he once told us of an incident that happened to him when he and another survivor were sitting on the stage waiting for their turn to speak at a Warsaw Ghetto memorial service. The speaker before him went on and on telling the audience on how many Germans he had killed. When he returned to his seat he gave Dad a nudge as if to say "now let's hear if you can beat that." Dad turned to him and answered "it's not how many Germans you killed — it's how many Jews did you manage to save." Then Dad stood up and made his speech.

When Dad did talk about the war years, I remember his phrases:

> How strange are the zigzags that life throws you. If I hadn't, for instance, taken a chance and sneaked into the "selected" group of people who were waiting for the Gestapo, with a list in his hands, to take them across to the First Ghetto where the "needed workers" were to go, we would have ended up going with the transport

to the concentration camps. Only by taking a gamble and moving quickly into the "selected" "needed workers" line, while the German had his face hidden as he lit a cigarette, did we become the "fortunate ones" for a little while longer.

Or when he spoke about the break-in at the military hospital to steal the weapons, he always said, "It happened so quickly that I did not realize the risks involved if we had gotten caught. When I think of it now — it was a mad plan. I must have been crazy and out of my mind to have undertaken it because had I stopped for a minute to think, I would certainly not have done it." Then he would turn to Mum and say: "And had I listened to you, and your Jewish fatalism of always saying 'what will happen to all will happen to us,' we would have ended up in the gas ovens together with the others." But by his brave and instinctive action of going ahead with his plan of stealing the weapons, twenty-six people managed to be saved, including us.

On our arrival in New Zealand, like all new immigrants everywhere, it took a while to get settled, find a job, accommodation and start making a living. But in time both Mum and Dad found work in their trades, Mum as a dressmaker and Dad as a carpenter.

A few years later he went into business on his own as an importer of fine art prints and picture framer. I think he found much satisfaction in his work — he could put down the tools and start writing or reading at his leisure, which he did very often. He was not interested in becoming rich, he just wanted to make a comfortable living. Mum used to say about Dad that he was virtually giving away his framed pictures. He would leave his stock for consignment at the shops, and I am sure that half the time he would forget what he gave to whom. Only on delivering new stock would he notice his previous pictures had gone from the display and been sold. He would then remind the proprietor that payment was due. He called this kind of businessman — Mr. Gunefsohn (Mr. Son of a Thief). There were also times when elderly clients would come to his workshop to have a picture of a grandchild framed, and in many instances he would not charge for them. I am sure he would have been the first to admit that he was no businessman. It just did not interest him. His mind was always somewhere else.

New Zealand itself was scenically beautiful and its people most friendly. But something was missing. He was starved for Jewish/Yiddish life. I imagine that for a man like dad who was thirsting for a Yiddish environment life in New Zealand must have been culturally quite empty. And most probably what kept him spiritually alive was his writing.

The Jewish community in Wellington was small and in time as more immigrants arrived a Yiddish speaking circle was formed. But he continued doing what he loved best — to write and contribute to the Yiddish journals and newspapers in Argentina, Australia and Israel.

When I left for Israel at the end of 1953, he saw it as a beginning and hope of all the family making aliya. In 1956 I received the very good news that Judy and I now had a baby brother — Samuel.

On his first trip to Israel in 1958, Dad was beaming as he stepped off the airplane. I have never seen him so happy. For the first time he met up with his brother Avram and sister Miriam, both of whom he had not seen for more than thirty years, since they left Grodno for Palestine as pioneers. It was a very emotional meeting — there was so much to talk about and catch up on. He visited his cousins in Karkur, his partisan friends, and the Fleisher family from Bielica — those kind Jews who so generously accepted us in their group in the forest when nobody else would because of the small child (me). They were for him the warm hearted simple *amcho* he loved and to whom he was forever grateful. They in turn honored and respected him and called him affectionately "Leibl der Grodner."

He became alive in Israel and tried to pack into those couple of weeks a lifetime of years gone by. In coming to Israel it was as though he had woken up from a long deep sleep. He just could not get enough of it — he was like a hungry man at a feast!

By 1972, with both my sister and I now living in Israel, there was no reason for him, Mum and Sam to remain in New Zealand. So in 1973 they made aliya and joined us. They purchased an apartment close to us in Ra'anana and Dad took to life in Israel with gusto. They enjoyed taking their little evening walks when the air was cooler and the scent of orange blossoms permeated the streets of Ra'anana. And as they strolled they would reminisce about their past turbulent life and how wonderful it was to sit this beautiful evening in this lovely garden and enjoy their last remaining years in our own land.

He now wrote much less, but still managed the odd story to the *Grodner Opklangen*. They were mainly memories from after the war and recollections of Grodno scenes and its people.

Dad loved nature in all its forms and in his writings always praised the forests that protected and saved him during the war. He wrote about them with such a longing and affection, mentioning that even as a youth he loved to wander into the forest in winter "when the snow had hardened and the trees with silver snow crowns shone in the cold dull sunlight."

It is to the credit of my sister Judy that she had the foresight to initiate Dad in making a short tape in 1982 telling us a little of his family history, his youthful years, and a small part of his experiences during the war.

Dad passed away on May 16, 1986 at the age of 76 and Mum on July 30, 2000 at the age of 88. Both were laid to rest in Kibbutz Tzora under the trees he loved. The tall pine tree that grows next to his grave covers it with delicate pine needles and accompanies him in his death as it protected him in his life.

Mum and Dad were the only survivors of the Holocaust from their families. Their entire families perished together with the rest of Grodno Jewry.

He wrote in "Forest and Bushes"[6] (Reminiscences of the Forests around Grodno):

> Only I alone, forest and bushes, know the score and secret… Only I alone know who from among the murdered Jews died with "Shma Yisrael"… who with a cry of "murderers" and who with a silent death fear in their eyes… solitary, hunted and deserted they breathed their last breath in terrible pain beside a root of a tree or a bush…
>
> Only today in distressing dreams, when the Germans are chasing me in the labyrinth of the Shuloif's [synagogue courtyard] narrow streets in the ghetto in order to pack me into the big shul and send me off to the transport — even today you suddenly reveal yourself to me my faithful saviors — forest and bushes — with your wide, thick green arms I happily vanish in you…
>
> I cherish and praise you forest and bushes that I survived in your shadows, and your darkest nights were my sunniest days, days that gave me courage and hope that my longed for hour will come…

Betty (Reizer) Broit

6   "Forest and Bushes," *Grodner Opklangen*, No. 11, September 1959.

PHOTOS

Note and Basia Reizer, parents of Leib Reizer

186   In the Struggle

Leib Reizer just after the war,
Grodno, 1944

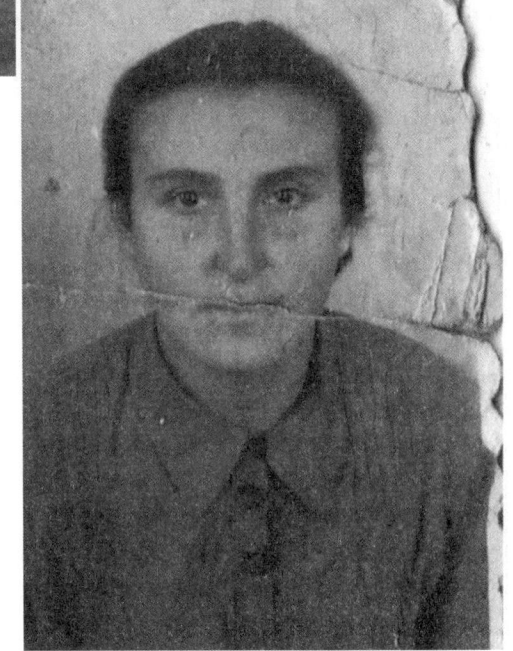

Fruma Reizer just after the war,
Grodno, 1944

PHOTOS 187

Betty Reizer in DP camp, UNRRA, Trofaiach, Austria, 1946

Leib Reizer by the partisan memorial in Gunskirchen, Austria, 1946

188 IN THE STRUGGLE

Betty and Judy Reizer in DP camp Trofaiach, Austria, 1946

Fruma and Leib Reizer with their children Betty and Judy in the DP camp, Trofaiach, Austria, 1946

Leib Reizer and his daughter Betty in
DP camp Bindermichl, Austria, 1946

Leib Reizer, 1947

Leib and Fruma Reizer at a Chanuka
party in the DP camp Geretstried,
Germany, 1947

190   IN THE STRUGGLE

Leib and Fruma Reizer with their daughter Judy in Rotorua,
New Zealand, 1954/1955

Leib Reizer and his son Samuel,
Wellington, New Zealand, 1958

Leib Reizer, with a group of children he met on the
way, Mount Zion, Jerusalem, 1958

Family in Israel, 1976: Front row: Samuel Reizer, Judy (Reizer) Amit, Leib Reizer, and Betty (Reizer) Broit; Back row: Adam Broit, Moshe Amit, father-in-law of Judy, and Fruma Reizer

Fruma and Leib Reizer with their daughter Betty (Reizer) Broit, Israel, 1982

Leib and Fruma Reizer, Ra'anana, Israel, 1985.
Leib passed away in 1986 and Fruma in 2000.